THE LETTER

A Play in Three Acts

by

W. SOMERSET MAUGHAM

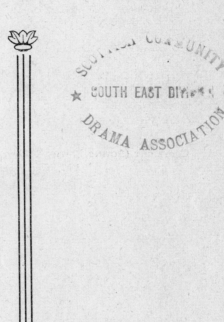

SAMUEL FRENCH LIMITED

LONDON

SAMUEL FRENCH, LTD.
26 SOUTHAMPTON STREET, STRAND, LONDON, W.C.2.

SAMUEL FRENCH, INC.
25 WEST 45TH STREET, NEW YORK, U.S.A.
7623 SUNSET BOULEVARD, HOLLYWOOD 46, CAL.

SAMUEL FRENCH (CANADA), LTD.
480 UVIVERSITY AVENUE, TORONTO

MADE AND PRINTED IN GREAT BRITAIN BY
RICHARD WHEWELL (BOLTON) LTD., FOLDS ROAD, BOLTON.

THE LETTER

Produced at the Playhouse Theatre, London, on February 24th, 1927, with the following cast of characters :

(In the order of their appearance) :

GEOFFREY HAMMOND	*S. J. Warmington*
LESLIE CROSBIE	*Gladys Cooper*
HEAD BOY	
JOHN WITHERS	*James Raglan*
ROBERT CROSBIE	*Nigel Bruce*
HOWARD JOYCE	*Leslie Faber*
ONG CHI SENG	*George Carr*
SIKH, SERGEANT OF POLICE	*Tom Mills*
MRS PARKER	*Marion Lind*
CHUNG HI	*A. G. Poulton*
CHINESE WOMAN	*Marie Chen Sing*
MRS JOYCE	*Clare Harris*

Chinese Boys, Malay Servants.

The Play produced by GERALD DU MAURIER

SYNOPSIS OF SCENES

The action of the play takes place on a plantation in the Malay Peninsula, and at Singapore.

ACT I.

The sitting-room of the Crosbie's bungalow. Midnight.

ACT II.

The visitors' room in the gaol at Singapore. Six weeks later.

ACT III.

SCENE 1.—A room in the Chinese quarter of Singapore. The same night.

SCENE 2.—The same as ACT I. Afternoon ; the next day.

(iii)

THE LETTER

ACT I.

SCENE.—*The sitting-room of the* CROSBIE'S *bungalow on a plantation in the Malay Peninsula. Midnight.*

The room is comfortably but quite simply furnished. There are three rattan armchairs, with cushions, one above the door R. *and one each side of a circular table at* R.C. *The chair on the* R. *of the table has an extending leg-rest. A writing-desk stands below the door* R. *with a small rattan chair pushed into it. There is an occasional table with a bowl of flowers* L. *of the* C. *opening. A cottage piano with a small rattan chair in front of it is in the corner up* L. *and a piece of music is open on the stand. Below the piano there is a bookcase. A long stool* R. *completes the furniture. A door in the* R. *wall leads to the bedroom. On the walls are water-colour pictures with here and there an arrangement of krises and parangs and some hunting trophies. There are rattan mats on the floor. The room is lit by two lamps, one on the piano and the other on the round table, on which also is* LESLIE'S *lace pillow. Across the back of the room runs a verandah, approached by steps from the garden, and divided from the room by a hand-rail, with a wide opening* C. *Rattan blinds, at present rolled up, can be lowered to separate the room from the verandah. A lamp hangs over the centre of the verandah.*

(See the Ground Plan at the end of the play.)

When the CURTAIN *rises, the lamps are lit. The sound of a shot is heard and a cry from* HAMMOND, *who is up* L.C. *He is seen staggering towards the verandah.* LESLIE, *with a revolver in her right hand, is standing below the chair* L. *of the table. She fires again.*

HAMMOND. Oh, my God ! *(He falls face down on the verandah.)*

*(*LESLIE *crosses to* L. *of the opening, turns, and stands over him. She fires several more shots in rapid succession into the prostrate body. There is a little click as she mechanically pulls the trigger and the six chambers are empty. She looks at the revolver and lets it drop from her hand ; then her eyes fall on the body, they grow enormous as though they would start out of her head, and a look of horror comes into her face. She gives a shudder as she looks at the dead man, and then, her gaze still fixed on the dreadful sight, backs into the room. There is an excited jabbering from the garden and* LESLIE *gives a start as she hears it. It is immediately followed by the appearance of the* HEAD-BOY *and another servant entering by the*

1

verandah steps R. *The* HEAD-BOY *is a small fat Chinaman of about forty. While he is speaking, two or three more Chinese servants wearing white trousers and singlets, and some Malays in sarongs, appear up the verandah steps* L.)

HEAD-BOY (*as he ascends the steps ; calling*). Missy ! Missy ! Whatchee matter ? I hear gunfire. (*He catches sight of the body.*) Oh !
(*The* BOY *with him speaks to him excitedly in Chinese.*)

LESLIE. Is he dead ?

HEAD-BOY. Missy ! Missy ! Who kill him ? (*He bends over and looks at the corpse.*) That Mr Hammond.

LESLIE. Is he dead ?

(*The* HEAD-BOY *kneels down and feels the man's face. The others stand round and chatter among themselves.*)

HEAD-BOY. Yes, I think him dead.

LESLIE (*breaking down* L.). Oh, my God !

HEAD-BOY (*rising*). Missy, what for you do that ?

LESLIE (*turning*). Do you know where the Assistant District Officer lives ?

HEAD-BOY. Mr Withers, Missy ? Yes, I savvy. He live jolly long way from here.

LESLIE. Fetch him.

HEAD-BOY. More better we wait till daylight, Missy.

LESLIE. There's nothing to be frightened of. Hassan will drive you over in the car. Is Hassan there ?

HEAD-BOY (*pointing to one of the Malays*). Yes, Missy.

LESLIE. Wake Mr Withers and tell him to come here at once. Say there's been an accident and Mr Hammond's dead.

HEAD-BOY. Yes, Missy.

LESLIE. Go at once.

(*The* HEAD-BOY *turns to* HASSAN *the chauffeur and gives him instructions in Malay to get out the car.* HASSAN *turns and exits down the steps* L.)

HEAD-BOY. I think more better we bring body in, Missy, and put him on bed in spare room.

LESLIE (*with a broken cry of anguish*). No.

HEAD-BOY. No can leave him here, Missy.

LESLIE. Don't touch it. When Mr Withers comes he'll say what's to be done.

HEAD-BOY (*moving into the room*). All right, Missy. I tell Ah Sing to wait here maybe. (*He stands* L. *of the table.*)

LESLIE. If you like. (*She pauses.*) I want Mr Crosbie sent for.

HEAD-BOY. Post office all closed up, Missy, no can telephone till tomollow morning.

LESLIE. What's the time ?

HEAD-BOY. I think, may be, twelve o'clock.

LESLIE. You must wake the man up at the post office as you go through the village, and he must get on to Singapore somehow or other. Or try at the police station. Perhaps they can get on.

HEAD-BOY. All light, Missy. I try.

LESLIE. Give the man two or three dollars. Whatever happens they must get on to him at once.

HEAD-BOY. If I catchee speak master, what thing I say, Missy?

LESLIE (*crossing below the table to the desk* R.). I'll write the message down for you. (*She sits at the desk, takes a sheet of paper and pencil.*)

HEAD-BOY. All light, Missy. You write.

LESLIE (*trying to write*). Oh, my hand! (*She puts the pencil down.*) I can't hold the pencil. (*She beats with her fist on the desk in anger with herself, and takes the pencil again. She writes a few words and then rises, paper in hand.*) Here's the message. (*She turns and moves* R.C.)

(*The* HEAD-BOY *moves down to* L. *of her.*)

That's the telephone number. Master is spending the night at Mr Joyce's house.

HEAD-BOY. I savvy. The lawyer.

LESLIE. They must ring and ring till they get an answer. They can give the message in Malay if they like. Read it and see if you understand. (*She holds the paper out towards him.*)

HEAD-BOY (*peering over the paper*). Yes, Missy. I understand.

LESLIE (*reading*). " Come at once. There's been a terrible accident. Hammond is dead." (*She gives him the paper.*)

HEAD-BOY. All light, Missy.

(*There is the sound of a car being started.*)

LESLIE. There's the car. Be quick now.

HEAD-BOY (*turning and moving up* C.). Yes, Missy.

(*He exits by the verandah steps* L. LESLIE *stands for a moment looking down on the floor. One or two* MALAY WOMEN *come softly up the verandah steps* L. *They look at the corpse and talk excitedly to each other in whispers.* LESLIE *becomes conscious of their presence.*)

LESLIE (*turning and moving up* C.). What do you want? Go away, all of you.

(*All exit silently down the verandah steps except* AH SING, *a Chinese boy.* LESLIE *gives the body a long look, then turns and exits into her bedroom by the door up* R., *which you hear her lock.* AH SING *enters* C., *moves to the circular table, helps himself to a cigarette and lights it. He then sits in the armchair* L. *of the table, crosses one leg over the other, and blows the smoke into the air.*)

CURTAIN.

When the CURTAIN *rises again it is three hours later. The scene is the same, but the body has been removed.* JOHN WITHERS, *a young man, neatly dressed in a white duck suit, is walking up and down the room. His topee is on the table up* L. *The* HEAD-BOY *enters* C. *and stands* R. *of the opening.*

HEAD-BOY.   My believe I hear motor-car on road.
WITHERS (*moving on to the verandah and listening*).   I don't. (*He turns irritably.*)   I can't imagine why he's so long.

(*There is the faint sound of a motor horn.*)

(*He turns to peer out again into the darkness.*)   Yes, by George ! That's a car. (*He turns and comes down into the room.*)   Thank the Lord for that.

(*The* HEAD-BOY *turns and exits down the verandah steps.*)

(*He crosses to the bedroom door up* R., *knocks and calls.*)   Mrs. Crosbie . . .   (*There is no answer and he knocks again.*)   Mrs Crosbie.
LESLIE (*off ; calling*).   Yes ?
WITHERS.   There's a car on the road.   That must be your husband. (*There is no reply to this.   He listens for a moment and then with a gesture of impatience crosses to the verandah.*)

(*The sound is heard of a car arriving.   It stops.*)

(*He calls.*)   Is that you, Crosbie ?
CROSBIE (*off ; calling*).   Yes.
WITHERS.   I thought you were never coming. (*He comes down into the room and stands* L.C.)

(CROSBIE *enters by the verandah steps.   He is a man of powerful build, forty years old, with a large sun-burned face ; he is dressed in khaki shorts, a shirt without a tie, a khaki coat and a broad-brimmed hat.*)

CROSBIE (*up* C.).   Where's Leslie ?
WITHERS.   She's in her room.   She's locked herself in.   She wouldn't see me till you came.
CROSBIE (*crossing to the door* R.).   What's happened ? (*He knocks urgently on the door and calls.*)   Leslie !   Leslie !

(*There is a moment's pause.* JOYCE *enters by the verandah steps.   He is a thin, spare, clean-shaven man of about forty-five.   He wears ducks and a topee.*)

JOYCE (*holding out his hand to* WITHERS).   My name is Joyce. Are you the A.D.O. ?

WITHERS (*shaking hands with* JOYCE).   Yes.   Withers.
JOYCE.   Crosbie was spending the night with us.   I thought I'd
better come along with him.
CROSBIE.   Leslie !   It's me !   Open the door !
WITHERS (*to* JOYCE).   Oh, are you the lawyer ?
JOYCE.   Yes.   Joyce and Simpson.
WITHERS.   I know.

(*The door* R. *is unlocked and slowly opened.* LESLIE *enters.   She
closes the door behind her and stands against it.*)

CROSBIE (*stretching out his hands as though to take her in his arms*).
Leslie.
LESLIE (*warding him off with a gesture*).   Oh, don't touch me.
CROSBIE.   What's happened ?   What's happened ?
LESLIE.   Didn't they tell you over the telephone ?
CROSBIE.   They said Hammond was killed.
LESLIE (*looking towards the verandah*).   Is he there still ?
WITHERS.   No.   I had the body taken away.

(LESLIE *looks at the three men with haggard eyes and then throws back
her head.*)

LESLIE.   He tried to rape me and I shot him.
CROSBIE.   Leslie !
WITHERS.   My God !
LESLIE.   Oh, Robert, I'm so glad you've come.
CROSBIE.   Darling !   Darling !

(LESLIE *throws herself in his arms and* ROBERT *clasps her to his heart.
Now at last she breaks down and sobs convulsively.*)

LESLIE.   Hold me tight.   Don't let me go.   I'm so frightened.
Oh, Robert, Robert.
CROSBIE.   It'll be all right.   There's nothing to be frightened
about.   Don't let yourself go to pieces.
LESLIE.   I've got you, haven't I ?   Oh, Robert, what shall I do ?
I'm so unhappy.
CROSBIE.   Sweetheart !
LESLIE.   Hold me close to you.
WITHERS.   Do you think you could tell us exactly what happened ?
LESLIE.   Now ?
CROSBIE.   Come and sit down, dear heart.   You're all in.

(*He leads her to the long chair* R. *of the table and she sinks into it with
exhaustion.*)

WITHERS.   I'm afraid it sounds awfully brutal, but my duty is . . .
LESLIE.   Oh, I know, of course.   I'll tell you everything I can.
I'll try to pull myself together. (*She looks up at* CROSBIE, *who is*

standing R. *of her.*) Give me your hankie. (*She takes a handker-chief out of his pocket and dries her eyes.*)

CROSBIE. Don't hurry yourself, darling. Take your time.

LESLIE (*forcing a smile to her lips*). It's so good to have you here.

CROSBIE. It's lucky Howard came along.

LESLIE. Oh, Mr Joyce, how nice of you ! (*She stretches out her hand.*) Fancy your coming all this way at this time of night !

JOYCE (*crossing to her and shaking hands*). Oh, that's all right.

LESLIE. How's Dorothy ?

JOYCE. Oh, she's very well, thank you.

LESLIE. I feel so dreadfully faint.

CROSBIE. Would you like a drop of whisky ?

LESLIE (*closing her eyes*). It's on the table.

(CROSBIE *crosses above the table* C. *to the small table up* L., *while* LESLIE *leans back in the chair, with her eyes closed, her face pale and wan.* JOYCE *eases softly towards* WITHERS.)

JOYCE (*in an undertone to* WITHERS). How long have you been here ?

WITHERS. Oh, an hour or more. I was fast asleep. My boy woke me up and said the Crosbies' head-boy was there and wanted to see me at once.

(CROSBIE *pours out a whisky and soda.*)

JOYCE. Did he tell you she'd shot him ?

WITHERS. Yes. When I got here Mrs Crosbie had locked herself in her room and refused to come out till her husband came.

JOYCE. Was Hammond dead ?

WITHERS. Oh, yes, he was just riddled with bullets.

JOYCE (*in a tone of faint surprise*). Oh !

WITHERS (*taking the revolver from his pocket*). Here's the revolver. All six chambers are empty.

(LESLIE *slowly opens her eyes and looks at the two men talking.* CROSBIE *turns and carries the whisky and soda below the table to* LESLIE. JOYCE *takes the revolver in his hand and looks at it.*)

JOYCE (*to* CROSBIE *as he crosses*). Is this yours, Bob ?

CROSBIE. Yes. (*He moves* R. *of* LESLIE *and supports her while she sips.*)

JOYCE (*to* WITHERS). Have you questioned the boys ?

WITHERS. Yes, they know nothing. They were asleep in their own quarters. They were awakened by the firing, and when they came here they found Hammond lying on the floor.

JOYCE. Where exactly ?

WITHERS (*pointing*). There. On the verandah under the lamp.

LESLIE. Thank you. I shall feel better in a minute. I'm sorry to be so tiresome.

JOYCE. Do you feel well enough to talk now ?

LESLIE. I think so.

CROSBIE. You needn't be in such a devil of a hurry. She's in no condition to make a long statement now.

JOYCE. It'll have to be made sooner or later.

LESLIE. It's all right, Robert, really. I feel perfectly well now.

JOYCE. I think we ought to be put in possession of the facts as soon as possible.

WITHERS. Take your time, Mrs Crosbie. After all, we're all friends here.

LESLIE. What do you want me to do ? If you've got any questions to ask, I'll do my best to answer them.

JOYCE (*moving and seating himself in the chair* L. *of the table*). Perhaps it would be better if you told us the whole story in your own way. Do you think you can manage that ?

LESLIE (*rising*). I'll try.

CROSBIE. What do you want to do ?

LESLIE. I want to sit upright. (*She sits again, upright on the chair extension, and hesitates a moment.*)

(*The eyes of all of them are on her face.*)

(*She addresses* WITHERS.) Robert was spending the night in Singapore, you know.

WITHERS. Yes, your boy told me that.

LESLIE. I was going in with him, but I wasn't feeling very well and I thought I'd stay here. I never mind being alone. (*With a half smile at* CROSBIE.) A planter's wife gets used to that, you know.

CROSBIE. That's true.

LESLIE. I had dinner rather late, and then I started working on my lace. (*She points to the pillow on which a piece of lace half made is pinned with little pins.*)

CROSBIE. My wife is rather a dab at lace-making.

WITHERS. Yes, I know. I've heard that.

LESLIE. I don't know how long I'd been working. It fascinates me, you know, and I lose all sense of time. Suddenly I heard a footstep outside and someone came up the steps of the verandah and said : " Good evening. Can I come in ? " I was startled, because I hadn't heard a car drive up.

WITHERS. Hammond left his car about a quarter of a mile down the road. It's parked under the trees. Your chauffeur noticed it as we were driving back.

JOYCE. I wonder why Hammond left his car there.

WITHERS. Presumably he did not want anyone to hear him drive up.

JOYCE. Go on, Mrs Crosbie.

LESLIE. At first I couldn't see who it was. I work in spectacles you know, and in the half-darkness of the verandah it was impossible for me to recognise anybody. " Who is it ? " I said. " Geoff Hammond." " Oh, of course, come in and have a drink," I said.

And I took off my spectacles.   I got up and shook hands with him.

JOYCE.   Were you surprised to see him ?

LESLIE.   I was, rather.   He hadn't been up to the house for ages, had he Robert ?

CROSBIE.   Three months at least, I should think.

LESLIE.   I told him Robert was away.   He'd had to go to Singapore on business.

WITHERS.   What did he say to that ?

LESLIE.   He said : " Oh, I'm sorry.   I felt rather lonely tonight, so I thought I'd just come along and see how you were getting on." I asked him how he'd come, as I hadn't heard a car, and he said he'd left it on the road because he thought we might be in bed and asleep and he didn't want to wake us up.

JOYCE.   I see.

LESLIE.   As Robert was away there wasn't any whisky in the room, but I thought the boys would be asleep, so I didn't call them ; I just went and fetched it myself.   Hammond mixed himself a drink and lit his pipe.

JOYCE.   Was he quite sober ?

LESLIE (*after a slight pause*).   I never thought about it.   I suppose he had been drinking, but just then it didn't occur to me.

JOYCE.   What happened ?

LESLIE.   Well, nothing very much ; I put on my spectacles again and went on with my work.   We chatted about one thing and another.   He asked me if Robert had heard that a tiger had been seen on the road two or three days ago.   It had killed a couple of goats and the villagers were in a state about it.   He said he thought he'd try to get it over the week-end.

CROSBIE.   Oh, yes, I know about that.   Don't you remember I spoke to you about it at tiffin yesterday.

LESLIE.   Did you ?   I believe you did.

WITHERS.   Fire away, Mrs Crosbie.

LESLIE.   Well, we were just chatting.   Then suddenly he said something rather silly.

JOYCE.   What ?

LESLIE.   It's hardly worth repeating.   He paid me a little compliment.

JOYCE.   I think perhaps you'd better tell us exactly what he said.

LESLIE.   He said : " I don't know how you can bear to disfigure yourself with those horrible spectacles.   You've got very pretty eyes indeed, you know, and it's too bad of you to hide them."

JOYCE.   Had he ever said anything of the sort to you before ?

LESLIE.   No, never.   I was a little taken aback, but I thought it best to take it quite lightly.   " I make no pretensions to being a raving beauty, you know," I said.   " But you are," he said.   It sounds awfully silly to repeat things like this.

JOYCE.   Never mind.   Please let us have his exact words.

LESLIE.   Well, he said : " It's too bad of you to try to make yourself look plain, but thank God you don't succeed." (*She gives the two strangers a faintly deprecating look.*) I shrugged my shoulders. I thought it rather impertinent of him to talk to me like that.

CROSBIE. I don't wonder.

JOYCE. Did you say anything ?

LESLIE. Yes, I said : " If you ask me point blank I'm bound to tell you that I don't care a row of pins what you think about me." I was trying to snub him, but he only laughed. " I'm going to tell you all the same," he said. " I think you're the prettiest thing I've seen for many a long year." " Sweet of you," I said, " but in that case I can only think you half-witted." He laughed again. He'd been sitting over there, and he got up and drew up a chair near the table I was working at. " You're not going to have the face to deny that you have the prettiest hands in the world," he said. That rather put my back up. In point of fact, my hands are not very good, and I'd just as soon people didn't talk about them. It's only an awful fool of a woman who wants to be flattered on her worst points.

CROSBIE. Leslie, darling. (*He takes one of her hands and kisses it.*)

LESLIE. Oh, Robert, you silly old thing.

JOYCE. Well, when Hammond was talking in that strain, did he just sit still with his arms crossed ?

LESLIE. Oh, no. He tried to take one of my hands. But I gave him a little tap. I wasn't particularly annoyed, I merely thought he was rather silly. I said to him : " Don't be an idiot. Sit down where you were before and talk sensibly, or else I shall send you home."

WITHERS. But, Mrs Crosbie, I wonder you didn't kick him out there and then.

LESLIE. I didn't want to make a fuss. You know, there are men who think it's their duty to flirt with a woman when they get the chance. I believe they think women expect it of them, and for all I know a good many do. But I'm not one of them, am I, Robert ?

CROSBIE. Far from it.

LESLIE. A woman only makes a perfect fool of herself if she makes a scene every time a man pays her one or two compliments. She doesn't need much experience of the world to discover that it means rather less than nothing. I didn't suspect for an instant that Hammond was serious.

JOYCE. When did you suspect ?

LESLIE. Then. What he said next. You see, he didn't move. He just looked at me straight in the face, and said : " Don't you know that I'm awfully in love with you ? "

CROSBIE. The cad.

LESLIE. " I don't," I answered. You see, it meant so little to me that I hadn't the smallest difficulty in keeping perfectly cool.

" I don't believe it for a minute," I said, " and even if it were true I don't want you to say it."

JOYCE.   Were you surprised ?

LESLIE.   Of course I was surprised.   Why, we've known him for seven years, Robert.

CROSBIE.   Yes, he came here after the war.

LESLIE.   And he's never paid me the smallest attention.   I didn't suppose he even knew what colour my eyes were.   If you'd asked me, I should have said I didn't begin to exist for him.

CROSBIE (*to* JOYCE).   You must remember that we never saw very much of him.

LESLIE.   When he first came here he was ill and I got Robert to go over and fetch him ;   he was all alone in his bungalow.

JOYCE.   Where was his bungalow ?

CROSBIE.   About six or seven miles from here.

LESLIE.   I couldn't bear the idea of his lying there without anyone to look after him, so we brought him here and took care of him till he was fit again.   We saw a certain amount of him after that, but we had nothing very much in common, and we never became very intimate.

CROSBIE.   For the last two or three years we've hardly seen him at all.   To tell you the truth, after all that Leslie had done for him when he was ill I thought he was almost too casual.

LESLIE.   He used to come over now and then to play tennis, and we used to meet him at other people's houses now and again.   But I don't think I'd set eyes on him for a month.

JOYCE.   I see.

LESLIE.   He helped himself to another whisky and soda.   I began to wonder if he'd been drinking.   Anyhow, I thought he'd had enough.   " I wouldn't drink any more if I were you," I said.   I was quite friendly about it.   I wasn't the least frightened or anything like that.   It never occurred to me that I couldn't manage him.   He didn't pay any attention to what I said.   He emptied his glass and put it down.   " Do you think I'm talking to you like this because I'm drunk ? " he asked in a funny abrupt way.   " That's the most obvious explanation, isn't it ? " I said.   It's awful having to tell you all this.   I'm so ashamed.   It's so disgraceful.

JOYCE.   I know it's hard.   But for your own sake I beg you to tell us the whole story now.

WITHERS.   If Mrs Crosbie would like to wait a little, I don't see any great harm in that.

LESLIE.   No, if I've got to tell it I'll tell it now.   What's the good of waiting ?   My head's simply throbbing.

CROSBIE.   Don't be too hard on her, Howard.

LESLIE.   He's being as kind as he can be.

JOYCE.   I hope so.   " That's the most obvious explanation," you said.

LESLIE.   " Well, it's a lie," he said.   " I've loved you ever since I

first knew you.   I've held my tongue as long as I could, and now
it's got to come out.   I love you.   I love you.   I love you."   He
repeated it just like that.

CROSBIE.   The swine.

LESLIE (*rising from her seat and standing*).   I got up and I put
away the pillow with my lace.   I held out my hand.   " Good
night," I said.   He didn't take it.   He just stood and looked at me
and his eyes were all funny.   " I'm not going now," he said.   Then I
began to lose my temper.   I think I'd kept it too long.   I think
I'm a very even-tempered woman, but when I'm roused I don't
care very much what I say.   " But, you poor fool," I cried at him,
" don't you know that I've never loved anyone but Robert, and even
if I don't love Robert you're the last man I should care for."   " What
do I care ? " he said.   " Robert's away."

CROSBIE.   The cur.   The filthy cur.   Oh, by God . . .

JOYCE.   Be quiet, Bob.

LESLIE.   That was the last straw, I was beside myself.   Even
then I wasn't frightened.   It never occurred to me he'd dare—he'd
dare . . .   I was just angry.   I thought he was just a filthy swine
to talk to me like that because he knew Robert was safely out of the
way.   " If you don't go away this minute," I said, " I shall call the
boys and have you thrown out."   He gave a filthy look.   " They're
out of earshot," he said.   I walked past him quickly.   I wanted to
get out on to the verandah, so that I could give the boys a call.   I
knew they'd hear me from there.   But he took hold of my arm and
swung me back.   " Let me go," I screamed.   I was furious.   " Not
much," he said.   " Not much.   I've got you now."   I opened my
mouth and shouted as loud as I could : " Boy ! Boy ! "   But he
puts his hand over it . . .   Oh, it's horrible.   I can't go on.   It's
asking too much of me.   It's so shameful, shameful.

CROSBIE.   Oh, Leslie, my darling.   I wish to God I'd never left
you.

LESLIE.   Oh, it was awful.   (*She sobs broken-heartedly.*)

JOYCE.   I beseech you to control yourself.   You've been wonderful up till now.   I know it's very hard, but you must tell us
everything.

LESLIE.   I didn't know what he was doing.   He flung his arms
round me.   He began to kiss me.   I struggled.   His lips were
burning, and I turned my mouth away.   " No, no, no ! " I screamed.
" Leave me alone.   I won't ! "   I began to cry.   I tried to tear
myself away from him.   He seemed like a madman.

CROSBIE.   I can't bear much more of this.

JOYCE.   Be quiet, Bob.

LESLIE.   I don't know what happened.   I was all confused.   I
was so frightened.   He seemed to be talking, talking.   He kept on
saying that he loved me and wanted me.   Oh, the misery !   He
held me so tight that I couldn't move.   I never knew how strong he
was.   I felt as weak as a rat.   It was awful to feel so helpless.   I'm

trying to tell you everything, but it's all in a blur. I felt myself growing weaker and weaker, and I thought I'd faint. His breath was hot on my face, and it made me feel desperately sick.

WITHERS. The brute.

LESLIE. He kissed me. He kissed my neck. Oh, the horror ! And he held me so tight that I felt I couldn't breathe. Then he lifted me right off my feet. I tried to kick him. He only held me tighter. Then I felt he was carrying me. He didn't say anything. I didn't look at him, but somehow I saw his face, and it was as white as a sheet and his eyes were burning. He wasn't a man any more, he was a savage ; I felt my heart pounding against my ribs . . . Don't look at me. I don't want any of you to look at me. It flashed across me that he was carrying me to the bedroom. Oh !

CROSBIE. If he weren't dead I'd strangle him with my own hands.

LESLIE. It all happened in a moment. He stumbled and fell. I don't know why. I don't know if he caught his foot in something or if it was just an accident. I fell with him. It gave me a chance. somehow his hold on me loosened and I snatched myself away from him. It was all instinctive ; It was the affair of a moment ; I didn't know what I was doing. I jumped up and I ran round the table. He was a little slow at getting up.

WITHERS. He had a game leg.

CROSBIE. Yes. He had his knee-cap smashed in the war.

LESLIE. Then he made a dash at me. There was a revolver on the table and I snatched it. I didn't even know I'd fired. I heard a report. I saw him stagger. He cried out. He said something. I don't know what it was. I was beside myself. I was in a frenzy. He lurched out of the room on to the verandah and I followed him. I don't remember anything. I heard the reports one after the other. I don't ask you to believe me, but I didn't even know I was pulling the trigger. I saw Hammond fall down. Suddenly I heard a funny little click and it flashed through my mind that I'd fired all the cartridges and the revolver was empty. It was only then that I knew what I'd done. It was as if scales dropped from my eyes, and all at once I caught sight of Hammond, and he was lying there in a heap.

CROSBIE (*moving to her and taking her in his arms*). My poor child.

LESLIE. Oh, Robert, what have I done ?

CROSBIE. You've done what any woman would have done in your place, only nine-tenths of them wouldn't have had the nerve.

JOYCE (*rising*). How did the revolver happen to be there ?

CROSBIE. I don't very often leave Leslie alone for the night, but when I do I feel safer if she's got a weapon handy. I saw that all the barrels were loaded before I left, and thank God I did.

LESLIE. That's all, Mr Withers. You must forgive me if I wouldn't see you when you came. But I wanted my husband.

WITHERS. Of course. May I say that I think you behaved magnificently. I'm fearfully sorry we had to put you to the ordeal of telling us all this. But I think Mr Joyce was right. It was much better that we should be in possession of all the facts immediately.

LESLIE. Oh, I know.

WITHERS. It's quite obvious the man was drunk, and he only got what he deserved.

LESLIE. And yet I'd give almost anything if I could bring him back to life. It's so awful to think that I killed him.

CROSBIE. It was an easy death for him. By God, if ever I've wanted to torture anyone . . .

LESLIE. No, don't, Robert, don't. The man's dead.

JOYCE. Could I see the body for a minute ?

WITHERS (*moving up* C.). Yes. I'll take you to where it is.

LESLIE (*with a little shudder*). You don't want me to come ?

JOYCE (*turning and moving up* C.). No, of course not. You stay here with Bob. We shall only be a minute.

(JOYCE *and* WITHERS *exit up* C.)

LESLIE. I'm so tired. I'm so desperately tired.

CROSBIE. I know you are, darling. I'd do anything to help you, there doesn't seem to be a thing I can do.

LESLIE. You can love me.

CROSBIE. I've always loved you with all my heart.

LESLIE. Yes, but now.

CROSBIE. If I could love you any more I would now.

LESLIE. You don't blame me ?

CROSBIE. Blame you ? I think you've been splendid. By God, you're a plucky little woman.

LESLIE (*tenderly*). This is going to give you an awful lot of anxiety, my dear.

CROSBIE. Don't think about me. I don't matter. Only think about yourself.

LESLIE. What will they do to me ?

CROSBIE. Do ? I'd like to see anyone talk of doing anything to you. Why, there isn't a man or a woman in the colony who won't be proud to know you.

LESLIE. I so hate the idea of everyone talking about me.

CROSBIE. I know, darling.

LESLIE. Whatever people say you'll never believe anything against me, will you ?

CROSBIE. Of course not. What should they say ?

LESLIE. How can I tell ? People are so unkind. They might easily say that he would never have made advances to me if I hadn't led him on.

CROSBIE. I think that's the last thing anyone who's ever seen you would dream of saying.

LESLIE. Do you love me very much, Robert ?

CROSBIE.   I can never tell you how much.

LESLIE.   We have been happy together all these years, haven't we ?

CROSBIE.   By George, yes ! We've been married for ten years
and it hardly seems a day. Do you know that we've never even
had a quarrel ?

LESLIE (*with a smile*). Who could quarrel with anyone as kind
and good-natured as you are ?

CROSBIE.   You know, Leslie, it makes me feel stupid and awkward
to say some things. I'm not one of those fellows with the gift of
the gab. But I do want you to know how awfully grateful I am to
you for all you've done for me.

LESLIE.   Oh, my dear, what are you talking about ?

CROSBIE.   You see, I'm not in the least clever. And I'm a great
ugly hulking devil. I'm not fit to clean your boots really. I never
knew at the beginning why you ever thought of me. You've been
the best wife a man ever had.

LESLIE.   Oh, what nonsense !

CROSBIE.   Oh, no, it isn't. Because I don't say much you mustn't
fancy I don't think a lot. I don't know how I've deserved all the
luck I've had.

LESLIE.   Darling ! It's so good to hear you say that.

(*He takes her in his arms and lingeringly kisses her mouth.* JOYCE
and WITHERS *enter* C. *Without self-consciousness* LESLIE *releases
herself from her husband's embrace and turns to the two men.*)

Wouldn't you like something to eat ? You must be perfectly
ravenous.

WITHERS (*moving down* L.). Oh, no, don't bother, Mrs Crosbie.

LESLIE (*crossing to* L.C.). It's no bother at all. I expect the boys
are about still, and if they're not I can easily make you a little
something myself.

JOYCE (*moving* R. *of* LESLIE). Personally, I'm not at all hungry.

LESLIE.   Robert ?

CROSBIE.   No, dear.

JOYCE.   In point of fact, I think it's about time we started for
Singapore.

LESLIE (*a trifle startled*). Now ?

JOYCE.   It'll be dawn when we get there. By the time you've had
a bath and some breakfast it'll be eight o'clock. We'll ring up the
Attorney-General and find out when we can see him. Don't you
think that's the best thing we can do, Withers ?

WITHERS.   Yes. I suppose so.

JOYCE.   You'll come with us, of course ?

WITHERS.   I think I'd better, don't you ?

LESLIE.   Shall I be arrested ?

JOYCE (*with a glance at* WITHERS). I think you're by way of being
under arrest now.

WITHERS.   It's purely a matter of form, Mrs Crosbie. Mr Joyce's idea is that you should go to the Attorney-General and give yourself up. Of course, all this is entirely out of my line. I don't know exactly what I ought to do.

LESLIE. Poor Mr Withers, I'm so sorry to give you all this trouble.

WITHERS. Oh, don't bother about me. The worst that can happen to me is that I shall get hauled over the coals for doing the wrong thing.

LESLIE (*with a faint smile*). And you've lost a good night's rest, too.

JOYCE. Well, we'll start when you're ready, my dear.

LESLIE. Shall I be imprisoned ?

JOYCE. That is for the Attorney-General to decide. I hope that after you've told him your story we shall be able to get him to accept bail. It depends on what the charge is.

CROSBIE. He's a very good fellow. I'm sure he'll do everything he can.

JOYCE. He must do his duty.

CROSBIE. What do you mean by that ?

JOYCE. I think it not unlikely that he'll say only one charge is possible, and in that case I'm afraid that an application for bail would be useless.

LESLIE. What charge ?

JOYCE. Murder.

(*There is a moment's pause. The only sign that* LESLIE *gives that the word startles her is the clenching of one of her hands. But it requires quite an effort for her to keep her voice level and calm.*)

LESLIE. I'll just go and change into a jumper. I won't be a minute. And I'll get a hat.

JOYCE. Oh, very well. You'd better go and give her a hand, Bob. She'll want someone to do her up.

LESLIE. Oh, no, don't bother. I can manage quite well by myself. A jumper doesn't have to be done up, my poor friend.

JOYCE. Doesn't it ? I forgot. I think you'd better go along all the same, old man.

LESLIE. I'm not thinking of committing suicide, you know.

JOYCE. I should hope not. The idea never occurred to me. I thought I'd like to have a word or two with Withers.

LESLIE (*crossing above* JOYCE *to the door* R.). Come along, Robert.

(*She exits up* R. CROSBIE *turns, moves up* R. *and follows her off.*)

WITHERS (*moving up* L.). By George ! That woman's a marvel.

JOYCE (*good-humouredly*). In what way ?

WITHERS (*easing* C.). I never saw anyone so calm in my life. Her self-control is absolutely amazing. She must have a nerve of iron

JOYCE (*moving down* L.). She has a great deal more character than I ever suspected.

WITHERS. You've known her a good many years, haven't you?

JOYCE. Ever since she married Crosbie. He's my oldest pal in the colony. But I've never known her very well. She hardly ever came into Singapore. I always found her very reserved, and I supposed she was shy. But my wife has been down here a good deal and she raves about her. She says that when you really get to know her she's a very nice woman.

WITHERS. Of course she's a very nice woman.

JOYCE (*with the faintest irony*). She's certainly a very pretty one.

WITHERS. I was very much impressed by the way in which she told that terrible story.

JOYCE. I wish she could have been a little more explicit here and there. It was rather confused towards the end.

WITHERS. My dear fellow, what do you expect? You could see that she was just holding on to herself like grim death. It seemed to me a marvel that she was so coherent. I say, what a swine that man was!

JOYCE. By the way, did you know Hammond?

WITHERS. Yes, I knew him a little. I've only been here three months, you know.

JOYCE. Is this your first job as A.D.O.?

WITHERS. Yes.

JOYCE. Was Hammond a heavy drinker?

WITHERS. I don't know that he was. He could take his whack, but I never saw him actually drunk.

JOYCE. Of course I've heard of him, but I never met him myself. He was by way of being rather a favourite with the ladies, wasn't he?

WITHERS. He was a very good-looking chap. You know the sort, very breezy and devil-may-care and generous with his money.

JOYCE. Yes, that is the sort they fall for.

WITHERS. I've always understood he was one of the most popular men in the colony. Before he hurt his leg in the war he held the tennis championship, and I believe he had the reputation of being the best dancer between Penang and Singapore.

JOYCE. Did you like him?

WITHERS. He was the sort of chap you couldn't help liking. I should have said he was a man who hadn't an enemy in the world.

JOYCE. Was he the sort of chap you'd expect to do a thing like this?

WITHERS. How should I know? How can you tell what a man will do when he's drunk?

JOYCE. My own opinion is that if a man's a blackguard when he's drunk he's a blackguard when he's sober.

WITHERS. What are you going to do, then?

JOYCE. Well, it's quite evident that we must find out about him.

(LESLIE *enters up* R. *She has changed her clothes and is carrying her hat. She is followed by* CROSBIE.)

LESLIE (*moving down* R., *below the table*). Well, I haven't been long, have I ?

JOYCE. I shall hold you up as an example to my Dorothy.

LESLIE. She's probably not half as slow as you are. I can always dress in a quarter of the time that Robert can.

CROSBIE (*crossing above the table to the verandah*). I'll just go and start her up.

WITHERS. Is there room for me, or shall I come along in the other car ?

LESLIE. Oh, there'll be plenty of room.

(CROSBIE *and* WITHERS *exit* C. LESLIE *is about to follow*.)

JOYCE (*moving* C. *to* LESLIE). There's just one question I'd like to ask you.

LESLIE (*stopping and turning*). Yes, what is it ?

JOYCE. Just now, when I was looking at Hammond's body, it seemed to me that some of the shots must have been fired when he was actually lying on the ground. It gives me the impression that you must have stood over him and fired and fired.

LESLIE (*putting her hand wearily on her forehead*). I was trying to forget for a minute.

JOYCE. Why did you do that ?

LESLIE. I didn't know I did.

JOYCE. It's a question you must expect to be asked.

LESLIE. I'm afraid you think I'm more cold-blooded than I am. I lost my head. After a certain time everything is all blurred and confused. I'm awfully sorry.

JOYCE. Don't let it worry you, then. I daresay it's very natural. I'm sorry to make a nuisance of myself.

LESLIE. Shall we go ?

JOYCE. Come on.

They exit C. *The* HEAD-BOY *enters* C. *and draws down the blinds that lead on to the verandah. He puts out the lights and exits* C., *leaving the room in darkness as—*

the CURTAIN *falls.*

ACT II.

SCENE.—*The visitors' room in the gaol at Singapore.   Six weeks later.*

It is a bare room of which we only see one corner.   In the wall R., *there is a barred window through which can be seen the prison yard and wall.   There are doors, down* R. *and* L.   *The only furniture is a large table of polished pitch pine and four plain chairs, one above the table, one each* R. *and* L. *of it, and one in the middle of the* L. *wall.*

(*See the Ground Plan at the end of the play.*)

When the CURTAIN *rises,* CROSBIE *is standing at the window. He wears an air of profound dejection.   He has on the clothes in which he is accustomed to walk over the estate—shorts and a khaki shirt ; he holds his shabby old hat in his hand.   He sighs deeply. The door* L. *opens and* JOYCE *enters.   He is followed by* ONG CHI SENG, *carrying a brief case.   He is a Cantonese, small but trimly built ; he is very neatly dressed in white ducks, patent-leather shoes and gay silk socks.   He wears a gold wrist-watch and invisible pince-nez.   From his breast-pocket protrudes a rolled-gold fountain pen.   He expresses himself with elaborate accuracy ; he has learned English as a foreign language, and speaks it perfectly ; but he has trouble with his rs, he always turns them into ls, and this gives his careful speech every now and then a faintly absurd air.*

CROSBIE (*turning*).   Howard.
JOYCE (*moving* C. *below the table*).   I heard you were here.

(ONG CHI SENG *moves above the table.*)

CROSBIE (*moving down* R.).   I'm waiting to see Leslie.
JOYCE.   I've come to see her too.
CROSBIE.   Do you want me to clear out ?
JOYCE (*moving* L. *of the table and above it*).   No, of course not. You go along and see her when they send for you, and then she can come here.

(ONG CHI SENG *eases* R. *and stands by the window.*)

CROSBIE.   I wish they'd let me see her here.   It's awful having to see her in a cell with that damned matron always there.
JOYCE.   I thought you'd probably look in at the office this morning.
CROSBIE (*crossing to* L. *of the table*).   I couldn't get away.   After all, the work on the estate has got to go on, and if I'm not there to look after it everything goes to blazes.   (*He draws the chair* L. *of the table away from it and sits.*)   I came into Singapore the moment I could.   Oh, how I hate that damned estate.
JOYCE (*seating himself on the up* L. *corner of the table*).   In point of fact, I don't think it's been a bad thing for you during these last few weeks to have some work that you were obliged to do.

18

CROSBIE.   I dare say not.   Sometimes I've thought I should go mad.

JOYCE.   You know you must pull yourself together, old man. You mustn't let yourself go to pieces.

CROSBIE.   Oh, I'm all right.

JOYCE.   You look as if you hadn't had a bath for a week.

CROSBIE.   Oh, I've had a bath all right.   I know my kit's rather grubby, but it's all right for tramping over the estate.   I came just as I was.   I hadn't the heart to change.

JOYCE.   It's funny that you should have taken it all so much harder than your missus.   She hasn't turned a hair.

(ONG CHI SENG *eases down* R.)

CROSBIE.   She's worth ten of me.   I know that.   I don't mind confessing it, I'm all in.   I'm like a lost sheep without Leslie.   It's the first time we've been separated for more than a day since we were married.   I'm so lonely without her.   (*He indicates* ONG CHI SENG.)   Who's that ?

JOYCE.   Oh, that's my confidential clerk, Ong Chi Seng.

(ONG CHI SENG *gives a little bow and smiles with a flash of white teeth.*)

CROSBIE.   What's he come here for ?

JOYCE.   I brought him with me in case I wanted him.   Ong Chi Seng is as good a lawyer as I am.   He took his degree in the University of Hong Kong, and as soon as he's learned the ins and outs of my business he's going to set up in opposition.

ONG CHI SENG.   Hi, hi.

JOYCE (*rising*).   Perhaps you'd better wait outside, Ong.   I'll call you if I want you.

ONG CHI SENG (*moving to the door* R.).   Very good, sir.   I shall be within earshot.

JOYCE.   It'll do if you're within call.

(ONG CHI SENG *exits* R.)

CROSBIE.   Oh, Howard, I wouldn't wish my worst enemy the agony that I've gone through during these horrible weeks.

JOYCE (*seating himself in the chair above the table*).   You look as if you hadn't had much sleep lately, old man.

CROSBIE.   I haven't.   I don't think I've closed my eyes the last three nights.

JOYCE.   Well, thank God it'll be over tomorrow.   By the way, you'll clean yourself up a bit for the trial, won't you ?

CROSBIE.   Oh, yes, rather.   I'm staying with you tonight.

JOYCE.   Oh, are you ?   I'm glad.   And you'll both come back to my house after the trial.   Dorothy's determined to celebrate.

CROSBIE.   I think it's monstrous that they should have kept Leslie in this filthy prison.

JOYCE. I think they had to do that.

CROSBIE. Why couldn't they let her out on bail ?

JOYCE. It's a very serious charge, I'm afraid.

CROSBIE. Oh, this red tape. She did what any decent woman would do in her place. Leslie's the best girl in the world. She wouldn't hurt a fly. Why, hang it all, man, I've been married to her for ten years ; do you think I don't know her ? God, if I'd got hold of that man I'd have wrung his neck, I'd have killed him without a moment's hesitation. So would you.

JOYCE. My dear fellow, everybody's on your side.

CROSBIE. Thank God nobody's got a good word to say for Hammond.

JOYCE. I don't suppose a single member of the jury will go into the box without having already made up his mind to bring in a verdict of " Not guilty."

CROSBIE. Then the whole thing's a farce. She ought never to have been arrested in the first place ; and then it's cruel, after all the poor girl's gone through, to subject her to the ordeal of a trial. There's not a soul I've met in Singapore, man or woman, who hasn't told me that Leslie was absolutely justified.

JOYCE. The Law is the Law. She admits that she killed the man. It is terrible, and I'm dreadfully sorry both for you and for her.

CROSBIE. I don't matter two straws.

JOYCE. But the fact remains that murder has been committed, and in a civilised community a trial is inevitable.

CROSBIE. Is it murder to exterminate noxious vermin ? She shot him as she would have shot a mad dog.

JOYCE. I should be wanting in my duty as your legal adviser if I didn't tell you that there is one point which causes me a little anxiety. If your wife had only shot Hammond once the whole thing would have been absolutely plain sailing. Unfortunately she fired six times.

CROSBIE. Her explanation is perfectly simple. Under the circumstances anyone would have done the same.

JOYCE. I dare say, and, of course, I think the explanation is very reasonable.

CROSBIE. Then what are you making a fuss about ?

JOYCE. It's no good closing our eyes to the facts. It's always a good plan to put yourself in another man's place, and I can't deny that if I were prosecuting for the Crown that is the point on which I would centre my enquiry.

CROSBIE. Why ?

JOYCE. It suggests not so much panic as uncontrollable fury. Under the circumstances which your wife has described one would expect a woman to be frightened out of her wits, but hardly beside herself with rage.

CROSBIE. Oh, isn't that rather far-fetched ?

JOYCE. I dare say. I just thought it was a point worth mentioning.

CROSBIE. I should have thought the really important thing was *Hammond's character, and, by heaven ! we've found out enough about him.

JOYCE. We've found out that he was living with a Chinese woman, if that's what you mean.

CROSBIE. Well, isn't that enough ?

JOYCE. I dare say it is. It was certainly an awful shock to his friends.

CROSBIE. She'd been actually living in his bungalow for the last eight months.

JOYCE. It's strange how angry that's made people. It's turned public opinion against him more than anything.

CROSBIE. I can tell you this, if I'd known it I'd never have dreamed of letting him come to my place.

JOYCE. I wonder how he managed to keep it so dark.

CROSBIE. Will she be one of the witnesses ?

JOYCE. I shan't call her. I shall produce evidence that he was living with her, and, public feeling being what it is, I think the jury will accept that as proof that Hammond was a man of notorious character.

(*A* SIKH SERGEANT OF POLICE *enters* R. *He is tall, bearded, dark, and dressed in blue.*)

SIKH (*to* CROSBIE). You come now, Sahib.

CROSBIE (*rising*). At last.

JOYCE (*rising*). You haven't got very long to wait now. In another twenty-four hours she'll be a free woman. Why don't you take her somewhere for a trip ? Even though we're almost dead certain to get an acquittal, a trial of this sort is anxious work, and you'll both of you want a rest.

CROSBIE. I think I shall want it more than Leslie. She's been a brick. Why, d'you know, when I've been to see her it wasn't I who cheered her up, it was she who cheered me up. By God, there's a plucky little woman for you, Howard !

JOYCE. I agree. Her self-control is amazing.

CROSBIE (*crossing to the door* R.). I won't keep her long. I know you're busy.

JOYCE. Thanks.

(CROSBIE *exits* R.)

(*To the* SIKH.)   Is my clerk outside, Sergeant ?

(*He has hardly spoken the words before* ONG CHI SENG *sidles in* R. *The* SIKH *exits.*)

Give me those papers you've got there, will you ?

ONG CHI SENG (*moving above the* R. *end of the table*). Yes, sir.

(He opens his brief case, extracts a bundle of papers and hands them to JOYCE.)

JOYCE (*taking the papers and seating himself above the table*).   That's • all, Ong.   If I want you, I'll call.

ONG CHI SENG.   May I trouble you for a few words private conversation, sir ?   (*He places his brief case on the table.*)

JOYCE (*smiling slightly*).   It's no trouble, Ong.

ONG CHI SENG.   The matter upon which I desire to speak to you, sir, is delicate and confidential.

JOYCE.   Mrs Crosbie will be here in five minutes.   Don't you think we might find a more suitable occasion for a heart-to-heart talk ?

ONG CHI SENG.   The matter on which I desire to speak with you, sir, has to do with the case of *R. v Crosbie*.

JOYCE.   Oh ?

ONG CHI SENG.   Yes, sir.

JOYCE.   I have a great regard for your intelligence, Ong.   I am sure I can trust you not to tell me anything that, as Mrs Crosbie's counsel, it is improper that I should be advised of.

ONG CHI SENG.   I think, sir, that you may rest assured of my discretion.   I am a graduate of the University of Hong Kong, and I won the Chancellor's Prize for English composition.

JOYCE.   Fire away, then.

ONG CHI SENG.   A circumstance has come to my knowledge, sir, which seems to me to put a different complexion on this case.

JOYCE.   What circumstance ?

ONG CHI SENG.   It has come to my knowledge, sir, that there is a letter in existence from the defendant to the unfortunate victim of the tragedy.

JOYCE.   I should not be at all surprised.   In the course of the last seven years I have no doubt that Mrs Crosbie often had occasion to write to Mr Hammond.

ONG CHI SENG.   That is very probable, sir.   Mrs Crosbie must have communicated with the deceased frequently, to invite him to dine with her, for example, or to propose a tennis game.   That was my first idea when the matter was brought to my notice.   This letter, however, was written on the day of the late Mr Hammond's death.

(There is an instant's pause. JOYCE, *a faint smile of amusement in his eyes, continues to look intently at* ONG CHI SENG.)

JOYCE.   Who told you this ?

ONG CHI SENG.   The circumstances were brought to my notice, sir, by a friend of mine.

JOYCE.   I have always known that your discretion was beyond praise, Ong Chi Seng.

ONG CHI SENG.   You will no doubt recall, sir, that Mrs Crosbie

has stated that until the fatal night she had had no communication
with the deceased for several weeks.

Joyce. Yes, I do.

Ong Chi Seng. This letter indicates in my opinion that her
statement was not in every respect accurate.

Joyce (*stretching out his hand for the letter*). Have you got the
letter ?

Ong Chi Seng. No, sir.

Joyce. Oh ! I suppose you know it's contents ?

Ong Chi Seng. My friend very kindly gave me a copy. Would
you like to peruse it, sir ?

Joyce. I should.

(Ong Chi Seng *takes from an inside pocket a bulky wallet. It is
filled with papers, Singapore dollar bills, and cigarette cards. He
searches among the papers.*)

Ah, I see you collect cigarette cards.

Ong Chi Seng. Yes, sir. I am happy to say that I have a
collection which is almost unique and very comprehensive. (*From
the confusion of papers he extracts a half-sheet of notepaper and places
it on the table in front of* Joyce.)

Joyce (*reading slowly, as though he could hardly believe his eyes*).
" Robert will be away for the night. I absolutely must see you. I
shall expect you at eleven. I am desperate, and if you don't come I
won't answer for the consequences. Don't drive up. Leslie."
What the devil does it mean ?

Ong Chi Seng. That is for you to say, sir.

Joyce. What makes you think that this letter was written by
Mrs Crosbie ?

Ong Chi Seng. I have every confidence in the veracity of my
informant, sir.

Joyce. That's more than I have.

Ong Chi Seng. The matter can very easily be put to the proof.
Mrs Crosbie will no doubt be able to tell you at once whether she
wrote such a letter or not.

(Joyce *rises and walks once or twice up and down the room. Then he
stops and faces* Ong Chi Seng.)

Joyce. It is inconceivable that Mrs Crosbie should have written
such a letter.

Ong Chi Seng. If that is your opinion, sir, the matter is, of
course, ended. My friend spoke to me on the subject only because
he thought, as I was in your office, you might like to know of the
existence of this letter before a communication was made to the
Public Prosecutor.

Joyce. Who has the original ?

Ong Chi Seng. You will remember, sir, no doubt, that after the
death of Mr Hammond, it was discovered that he had had relations

with a Chinese woman. The letter is at present in her possession.

(*They face each other for a moment silently.*)

JOYCE. I am obliged to you, Ong. I will give the matter my consideration.

ONG CHI SENG. Very good, sir. Do you wish me to make a communication to that effect to my friend ? (*He picks up his brief case.*)

JOYCE. I dare say it would be as well if you kept in touch with him.

ONG CHI SENG (*moving to the door* R.). Yes, sir.

(*He exits* R. JOYCE *reads through the letter once more with knitted brows. Footsteps are heard off* R., *and he realises that* LESLIE *is coming. He places the copy of the letter among the papers on the table.* LESLIE *enters* R., *followed by the Matron,* MRS PARKER, *a stout middle-aged Englishwoman in a white dress.* LESLIE *is very simply and neatly dressed ; her hair is done with her habitual care ; she is cool and self-possessed.* JOYCE *rises and moves* L. *to below the table.*)

JOYCE. Good morning, Mrs Crosbie.

(LESLIE *moves* C. *graciously. She holds out her hand as calmly as though she were receiving him in her drawing-room.*)

LESLIE (*shaking hands with* JOYCE). How do you do ? I wasn't expecting you so early.

JOYCE. How are you doday ?

LESLIE. I'm in the best of health, thank you. This is a wonderful place for a rest cure. And Mrs Parker looks after me like a mother.

JOYCE. How do you do, Mrs Parker ?

MRS PARKER. Very well, thank you, sir. This I can't help saying, Mrs Crosbie, no one could be less trouble than what you are. I shall be sorry to lose you, and that's a fact.

LESLIE (*with a gracious smile*). You've been very kind to me, Mrs Parker.

MRS PARKER. Well, I've been company for you. When you're not used to it, it's lonely-like in a place like this. It's a shame they ever put you here, if you want to know what I think about it.

JOYCE. Well, Mrs Parker, I dare say you won't mind leaving us. Mrs Crosbie and I have got business to talk about.

MRS PARKER (*turning and moving to the door* R.). Very good, sir.

(*She exits* R.)

LESLIE. Sometimes she drives me nearly mad, she's so chatty, poor dear. Isn't it strange how few people there are who can ever realise that you may be perfectly satisfied with your own company ?

JOYCE. You must have had plenty of that lately.

LESLIE.   I've read a great deal, you know, and I've worked at my lace.

JOYCE.   I need hardly ask if you've slept well.

LESLIE.   I've slept like a top.   The time has really passed very quickly.

JOYCE.   It's evidently agreed with you.   You're looking very much better and stronger than a few weeks ago.

LESLIE.   That's more than poor Robert is.   He's a wreck, poor darling.   I'm thankful for his sake that it'll all be over tomorrow. I think he's just about at the end of his tether.

JOYCE.   He's very much more anxious about you than you appear to be about yourself.

LESLIE.   Won't you sit down ?

JOYCE (*moving* L. *above the table*).   Thank you.   (*He sits above the table.*)

LESLIE (*crossing and sitting* L. *of the table*).   I'm not exactly looking forward to the trial, you know.

JOYCE.   One of the things that has impressed me is that each time you've told your story you've told it in exactly the same words. You've never varied a hair's breadth.

LESLIE (*gently chaffing him*).   What does that suggest to your legal mind ?

JOYCE.   Well, it suggests either that you have an extraordinary memory or that you're telling the plain, unvarnished truth.

LESLIE.   I'm afraid I have a very poor memory.

JOYCE.   I suppose I'm right in thinking that you had no communication with Hammond for several weeks before the catastrophe ?

LESLIE (*with a friendly little smile*).   Oh, quite.   I'm positive of that.   The last time we met was at a tennis party at the McFarrens'. I don't think I said more than two words to him.   They have two courts, you know, and we didn't happen to be in the same sets.

JOYCE.   And you hadn't written to him ?

LESLIE.   Oh, no.

JOYCE.   Are you perfectly certain of that ?

LESLIE.   Oh, perfectly.   There was nothing I should write to him for except to ask him to dine, or play tennis and I hadn't done either for months.

JOYCE.   At one time you'd been on fairly intimate terms with him. How did it happen that you had stopped asking him to anything ?

LESLIE (*with a little shrug of the shoulders*).   One gets tired of people.   We hadn't anything very much in common.   Of course, when he was ill, Robert and I did everything we could for him, but the last year or two he's been quite well.   And he was very popular. He had a good many calls on his time, and there didn't seem to be any need to shower invitations upon him.

JOYCE.   Are you quite certain that was all ?

(LESLIE *hesitates for a moment and reflectively looks down.*)

LESLIE.   Well, of course, I knew about the Chinese woman.   I'd
actually seen her.
JOYCE.   Oh !   You never mentioned that.
- LESLIE.   It wasn't a very pleasant thing to talk about.   And I
knew you'd find out for yourselves soon enough.   Under the circumstances I didn't think it would be very nice of me to be the
first to tell you about his private life.
JOYCE.   What was she like ?

(LESLIE *gives a slight start and a hard look suddenly crosses her face.*)

LESLIE.   Oh, horrible.   Stout and painted and powdered.
Covered with gold chains and bangles and pins.   Not even young.
She's older than I am.
JOYCE.   And it was after you knew about her that you ceased
having anything to do with Hammond ?
LESLIE.   Yes.
JOYCE.   But you said nothing about it to your husband.
LESLIE.   It wasn't the sort of thing I cared to talk to Robert about.

(JOYCE *watches her for a moment.   Any suggestion of emotion that
showed itself on her face when she spoke of the Chinese woman has
left it and she is now once more cool and self-possessed.*)

JOYCE.   I think I should tell you that there is in existence a letter
in your handwriting from you to Geoff Hammond.
LESLIE.   In the past I've often sent him little notes to ask him to
something or other or to get me something when I knew he was
going into Singapore.
JOYCE.   This letter asks him to come and see you because Robert
was going to Singapore.
LESLIE (*smiling*).   That's impossible.   I never did anything of the
kind.
JOYCE (*taking the letter from among his papers*).   You'd better read
it for yourself.   (*He hands her the letter.*)
LESLIE (*taking it and glancing quickly at it*).   That's not my handwriting.   (*She gives it back.*)
JOYCE.   I know.   It's said to be an exact copy of the original.

(LESLIE *takes the letter again and now reads the words.   And as she
reads a horrible change comes over her.   He colourless face grows
dreadful to look at.   The flesh seems on a sudden to fall away and
her skin is tightly stretched over the bones.   She stares at* JOYCE
with eyes that start from their sockets.)

LESLIE (*in a whisper*).   What does it mean ?
JOYCE.   That is for you to say.
LESLIE.   I didn't write it.   I swear I didn't write it.
JOYCE.   Be very careful what you say.   If the original is in your
handwriting, it would be useless to deny it.
LESLIE.   It would be forgery.

Joyce. It would be difficult to prove that. It would be easy to prove that it was genuine.

(*A shiver passes through* Leslie's *body. She takes out a handkerchief and wipes the palms of her hands. She looks at the letter again.*)

Leslie (*returning the letter*). It's not dated. If I had written it and forgotten all about it, it might have been written years ago. If you'll give me time I'll try to remember the circumstances.

Joyce. I noticed there was no date. If this letter were in the hands of the prosecution they would cross-examine your house-boys. They would soon find out whether someone took a letter to Hammond on the day of his death.

(Leslie *clasps her hands violently and sways on her chair so that you might think she would faint.*)

Leslie. I swear to you that I did not write that letter.

Joyce. In that case we need not go into the matter further. If the person who possesses this letter sees fit to place it in the hands of the prosecution you will be prepared . . .

(*There is a long pause.* Joyce *waits for* Leslie *to speak, but she stares straight in front of her.*)

If you have nothing more to say to me, I think I'll be getting back to my office.

Leslie (*still not looking at him*). What would anyone who read the letter be inclined to think that it meant ?

Joyce. He'd know that you had told a deliberate lie.

Leslie. When ?

Joyce. When you stated definitely that you had had no communication with Hammond for at least six weeks.

Leslie. The whole thing has been a terrible shock to me. The events of that horrible night have been a nightmare. It's not very strange if one detail has escaped my memory.

Joyce. Your memory has reproduced very exactly every particular of your interview with Hammond. It is very strange that you should have forgotten so important a point as that he came to the bungalow on the night of his death at your express desire.

Leslie. I hadn't forgotten.

Joyce. Then why didn't you mention it ?

Leslie. I was afraid to. I thought you'd none of you believe my story if I admitted that he'd come at my invitation. I daresay it was very stupid of me. I lost my head, and after I'd once said that I'd had no communication with Hammond I was obliged to stick to it.

Joyce. You will be required to explain then why you asked Hammond to come to you when Robert was away for the night.

Leslie (*with a break in her voice*). It was a surprise I was preparing for Robert's birthday. I knew he wanted a new gun, and, you know,.

I'm dreadfully stupid about sporting things. I wanted to talk to Geoff about it. I thought I'd get him to order it for me.

JOYCE. Perhaps the terms of the letter are not very clear to your recollection. Will you have another look at it ?

LESLIE (*quickly drawing back*). No, I don't want to.

JOYCE. Then I must read it to you. " Robert will be away for the night. I absolutely must see you. I shall expect you at eleven. I am desperate, and if you don't come I won't answer for the consequences. Don't drive up. Leslie." Does it seem to you the sort of letter a woman would write to a rather distant acquaintance because she wanted to consult him about buying a gun ?

LESLIE. I dare say it's rather extravagant and emotional. I do express myself like that, you know. I'm quite prepared to admit it's rather silly.

JOYCE. I must have been very much mistaken. I always thought you a very reserved and self-possessed woman.

LESLIE. And after all, Geoff Hammond wasn't quite a distant acquaintance. When he was ill I nursed him like a mother.

JOYCE. By the way, did you call him Geoff ?

LESLIE. Everybody did. He wasn't the kind of man anyone would think of calling Mr Hammond.

JOYCE. Why did you ask him to come at so late an hour ?

LESLIE (*recovering her self-possession*). Is eleven very late ? He was always dining somewhere or other. I thought he'd look in on his way home.

JOYCE. And why did you ask him not to drive up ?

LESLIE (*with a shrug of the shoulder*). You know how Chinese boys gossip. If they'd heard him come, the last thing they'd have ever thought was that he was there for a perfectly innocent purpose.

(JOYCE *rises and walks once or twice up and down the room. Then, leaning over the back of his chair, he speaks in a tone of deep gravity.*)

JOYCE. Mrs Crosbie, I want to talk to you very, very seriously. This case was comparatively plain sailing. There was only one point that seemed to me to require explanation. So far as I could judge, you had fired no less than four shots into Hammond when he was lying on the ground. It was hard to accept the possibility that a delicate, frightened woman, of gentle nurture and refined instincts, should have surrendered to an absolutely uncontrollable frenzy. But, of course, it was admissible. Although Geoffrey Hammond was much liked, and on the whole thought highly of, I was prepared to prove that he was the sort of man who might be guilty of the crime which in justification of your act you accused him of. The fact, which was discovered after his death, that he had been living with a Chinese woman gave us something very definite to go upon. That robbed him of any sympathy that might have been felt for him. We made up our minds to make every use of the odium that such a connection cast upon him in the minds of respectable people. I told your husband just now that I was certain of an acquittal, and I wasn't just telling him that to cheer him up. I do not believe the jury would have left the box.

(*They look into each other's eyes. LESLIE is strangely still. She is like a bird paralysed by the fascination of a snake.*)

But this letter has thrown an entirely different complexion on the case. I am your legal adviesr. I shall represent you in court. I take your story as you tell it to me, and I shall conduct your defence according to its terms. It may be that I believe your statements, or it may be that I doubt them. The duty of counsel is to persuade the jury that the evidence placed before them is not such as to justify them in bringing in a verdict of guilty, and any private opinion he may have of the innocence or guilt of his client is entirely beside the point.

LESLIE. I don't know what you're driving at.

JOYCE. You're not going to deny that Hammond came to your house at your urgent and, I may even say, hysterical invitation ?

(LESLIE *does not answer for a moment. She seems to consider.*)

LESLIE. They can prove that the letter was taken to his bungalow by one of the house-boys. He rode over on his bicycle.

JOYCE. You mustn't expect other people to be stupider than you. The letter will put them on the track of suspicions that have entered nobody's head. I will not tell you what I personally thought when I read it. I do not wish you to tell me anything but what is needed to save your neck.

(LESLIE *crumples up suddenly and slips from her chair to the floor in a dead faint before* JOYCE *can catch her. He glances round the room for water, but there is none to be seen. He looks towards the door, but will not call for help. He does not wish to be disturbed. He moves and kneels down on one knee beside her, waiting for her to recover, and in a few moments she opens her eyes.*)

JOYCE. Keep quite still. You'll be better in a minute.

LESLIE (*raising herself with his help to a sitting position*). Don't let anyone come.

JOYCE (*supporting her*). No, no.

LESLIE (*clasping her hands and looking up at him appealingly*). Mr Joyce, you won't let them hang me. (*She begins to cry hysterically.*)

JOYCE (*trying to calm her ; in undertones*). Sh ! Sh ! Don't make a noise. Sh ! Sh ! It's all right. Don't, don't, don't. For goodness sake pull yourself together.

LESLIE. Give me a minute. (*She makes an effort to regain her self-control, and soon she is once more calm.*)

JOYCE (*with almost unwilling admiration*). You've got pluck. I think no one could deny that.

LESLIE.   Let me get up now.   It was silly of me to faint.

(JOYCE *helps her to her feet and leads her to the chair* L. *of the table, and she sinks down wearily.*)

JOYCE.   Do you feel a little better ?

LESLIE (*with her eyes closed*).   Don't talk to me for a moment or two.

JOYCE.   Very well.   (*He moves up* R. *to the window and stands gazing out of it.*)

(*There is a pause.*)

LESLIE (*with a little sigh*).   I'm afraid I've made rather a mess of things.

JOYCE (*turning*).   I'm sorry.

LESLIE.   For Robert, not for me.   You distrusted me from the beginning.

JOYCE (*moving down* R.).   That's neither here nor there.

(LESLIE *gives him a glance and then looks down.*)

LESLIE.   Isn't it possible to get hold of the letter ?

JOYCE (*with a frown to conceal his embarrassment*).   I don't think anything would have been said to me about it if the person in whose possession it is, was not prepared to sell it.

LESLIE.   Who's got it ?

JOYCE.   The Chinese woman who was living in Hammond's house.

(LESLIE *instinctively clenches her hands ; but again controls herself.*)

LESLIE.   Does she want an awful lot for it ?

JOYCE (*crossing* C., *below the table*).   I imagine that she has a pretty shrewd idea of its value.   I doubt if it would be possible to get hold of it except for a very large sum.

LESLIE (*hoarsely*).   Are you going to let me be hanged ?

JOYCE (*with some irritation*).   Do you think it's so simple as all that to secure possession of an unwelcome piece of evidence ?

LESLIE.   You say the woman is prepared to sell it.

JOYCE.   But I don't know that I'm prepared to buy it.

LESLIE.   Why not ?

JOYCE.   I don't think you know what you're asking me.   Heaven knows, I don't want to make phrases, but I've always thought I was by way of being an honest man.   You're asking me to do something that is no different from suborning a witness.

LESLIE (*her voice rising*).   Do you mean to say you can save me and you won't ?   What harm have I ever done you ?   You can't be so cruel.

JOYCE.   I'm sorry it sounds cruel.   I want to do my best for you, Mrs Crosbie.   A lawyer has a duty not only to his client, but to his profession.

LESLIE (*with dismay*).   Then what is going to happen to me ?

JOYCE (*very gravely*).   Justice must take its course.

(LESLIE *grows very pale. A little shudder passes through her body. When she answers her voice is low and quiet.*)

LESLIE.   I put myself in your hands.   Of course, I have no right to ask you to do anything that isn't proper.   I was asking more for Robert's sake than for mine.   But if you knew everything, I believe you'd think I was deserving of your pity.

JOYCE.   Poor old Bob, it'll nearly kill him.   He's utterly unprepared.

LESLIE.   If I'm hanged it certainly won't bring Geoff Hammond back to life again.

(*There is a moment's silence while* JOYCE *reflects upon the situation.*)

JOYCE (*almost to himself*).   Sometimes I think that when we say our honour prevents us from doing this or that we deceive ourselves, and our real motive is vanity.   I ask myself, what really is the explanation of that letter ?   I daren't ask you.   It's not fair to you to conclude from it that you killed Hammond without provocation. (*With emotion.*)   It's absurd how fond I am of Bob.   You see, I've known him for so long.   His life may very well be ruined too.

LESLIE.   I know I have no right to ask you to do anything for me, but Robert is so kind and simple and good.   I think he's never done anyone any harm in his life.   Can't you save him from this bitter pain and this disgrace ?

JOYCE.   You mean everything in the world to him, don't you ?

LESLIE.   I suppose so.   I'm very grateful for the love he's given me.

JOYCE (*making his resolution*).   I'm going to do what I can for you.

(LESLIE *gives a little gasp of relief.*)

But don't think I don't know I'm doing wrong.   I am.   I'm doing it with my eyes open.

LESLIE (*rising*).   It can't be wrong to save a suffering woman. You're doing no harm to anybody else.

JOYCE.   You don't understand.   It's only natural.   Let's not discuss that.   Do you know anything about Bob's circumstances ?

LESLIE.   He has a good many tin shares and a part interest in two or three rubber estates.   I suppose he could raise money.

JOYCE.   He would have to be told what it was for.

LESLIE.   Will it be necessary to show him the letter ?

JOYCE.   Don't you want him to see it ?

LESLIE.   No.

JOYCE.   I shall do everything possible to prevent him from seeing it till after the trial.   He will be an important witness.   I think it very necessary that he should be as firmly convinced of your innocence as he is now.

LESLIE.   And afterwards ?

JOYCE.   I'll still do my best for you.

LESLIE.   Not for my sake—for his.   If he loses his trust in me he loses everything.

JOYCE (*moving to the door* R.).   It's strange that a man can live with a woman for ten years and not know the first thing about her. It's rather frightening.

LESLIE.   He knows that he loves me.   Nothing else matters.

JOYCE (*opening the door* R. *and calling*).   Mrs Parker, I'm just going.   (*He leaves the door open, turns and moves* C.)

(MRS PARKER *enters* R.)

MRS PARKER.   Gracious, how white you look, Mrs Crosbie. Mr Joyce hasn't been upsetting you, has he ?   You look like a ghost.

LESLIE (*smiling graciously, with an instinctive resumption of her social manner*).   No, he's been kindness itself.   I daresay the strain is beginning to tell on me a little.   (*She holds out her hand to* JOYCE.) Good-bye.   It's good of you to take all this trouble for me.   I can't begin to tell you how grateful I am.

JOYCE (*shaking hands with her*).   I shan't see you again till just before the trial tomorrow.

LESLIE.   I've got a lot to do before then.   I've been making Mrs Parker a lace collar, and I want to get it done before I leave here.

MRS PARKER.   It's so grand.   I shall never be able to bring myself to wear it.   She makes beautiful lace, you'd be surprised.

JOYCE.   I know she does.

LESLIE (*crossing below them to the door* R.).   I'm afraid it's my only accomplishment.

(*She exits* R.)

JOYCE.   Good morning, Mrs Parker.

MRS PARKER.   Good morning, sir.

(*She exits* R.   JOYCE *moves above the table and begins to collect his papers together.   There is a knock at the door* R.)

JOYCE.   Come in.

(*The door* R. *is opened, and* ONG CHI SENG *enters.*)

ONG CHI SENG.   I desire to remind you, sir, that you have an appointment with Mr Reed, of Reed and Pollock, at twelve thirty.

JOYCE (*glancing at his watch*).   He'll have to wait.

ONG CHI SENG.   Very good, sir.   (*He crosses to the door* L., *and is about to go out, then stops and turns, as though on an afterthought.*)   Is there anything further you wish me to say to my friend, sir ?

JOYCE.   What friend ?

ONG CHI SENG.   About the letter which Mrs Crosbie wrote to Hammond, deceased, sir.

JOYCE (*very casually*).   Oh, I'd forgotten about that.   I mentioned it to Mrs Crosbie and she denies having written anything of the sort.   It's evidently a forgery.   (*He takes out the copy letter from the papers in front of him and offers it* ONG CHI SENG.)

ONG CHI SENG (*ignoring the gesture*).   In that case, sir, I suppose there would be no objection if my friend delivered the letter to the Public Prosecutor.

JOYCE (*seating himself above the table*).   None.   But I don't quite see what good that would do your friend.

ONG CHI SENG (*crossing to* R. *of the table*).   My friend thought it was his duty, sir, in the interests of justice.

JOYCE (*grimly*).   I'm the last man in the world to interfere with anyone who wishes to do his duty, Ong.

ONG CHI SENG (*moving above the table to* R. *of* JOYCE).   I quite understand, sir, but from my study of the case, *R. v. Crosbie*, I am of the opinion that the production of such a letter would be damaging to our client.

JOYCE.   I have always had a high opinion of your legal acumen, Ong Chi Seng.

ONG CHI SENG.   It has occurred to me, sir, that if I could persuade my friend to induce the Chinese woman who has the letter to deliver it into our hands it would save a great deal of trouble.

JOYCE.   I suppose your friend is a business man.   Under the circumstances do you think he would be induced to part with the letter ?

ONG CHI SENG.   He has not got the letter.

JOYCE.   Oh, has he got a friend, too ?

ONG CHI SENG.   The Chinese woman has got the letter.   He is only a relation of the Chinese woman.   She is an ignorant woman ; she did not know the value of the letter till my friend told her.

JOYCE.   What value did he put on it ?

ONG CHI SENG.   Ten thousand dollars, sir.

JOYCE.   Good God !   Where on earth do you suppose Mrs Crosbie can get ten thousand dollars ?   I tell you the letter's a forgery.

ONG CHI SENG.   Mr Crosbie owns an eighth share of the Bekong Rubber Estate, and a sixth share of the Kelanton River Rubber Estate.   I have a friend who will lend him the money on the security of his properties.

JOYCE.   You have a large circle of acquaintances, Ong.

ONG CHI SENG.   Yes, sir.

JOYCE.   Well, you can tell them all to go to Hell.   I would never advise Mr Crosbie to give a penny more than five thousand for a letter that can be very easily explained.

ONG CHI SENG.   The Chinese woman does not want to sell the letter, sir.   My friend took a long time to persuade her.   It is useless to offer her less than the sum mentioned.

JOYCE.   Ten thousand dollars is an awful lot.

ONG CHI SENG.   Mr Crosbie will certainly pay it rather than see his wife hanged by the neck, sir.

JOYCE.   Why did your friend fix upon that particular amount ?

ONG CHI SENG.   I will not attempt to conceal anything from you, sir.   Upon making enquiry, sir, my friend came to the conclusion that ten thousand dollars was the largest sum Mr Crosbie could possibly get.

JOYCE.   Ah, that is precisely what occurred to me.   Well, I will speak to Mr Crosbie.

ONG CHI SENG.   Mr Crosbie is still here, sir.

JOYCE.   Oh !   What's he doing ?

ONG CHI SENG.   We have only a very short time, sir, and the matter, in my opinion, brooks of no delay.

JOYCE.   In that case be brief, Ong.

ONG CHI SENG.   It occurred to me that you would wish to speak to Mr Crosbie and, therefore, I took the liberty of asking him to wait.   If it would be convenient for you to speak to him now, sir, I could impart your decision to my friend when I have my tiffin.

JOYCE.   Where is the Chinese woman now ?

ONG CHI SENG.   She is staying in the house of my friend, sir.

JOYCE.   Will she come to my office ?

ONG CHI SENG.   I think it more better you go to her, sir.   I can take you to the house tonight, and she will give you the letter.   She is a very ignorant woman and she does not understand cheques.

JOYCE.   I wasn't thinking of giving her a cheque.   I should bring banknotes with me.

ONG CHI SENG.   It would only be waste of time to bring less than ten thousand dollars, sir.

JOYCE.   I quite understand.

ONG CHI SENG (*moving to the door* R.).   Shall I tell Mr Crosbie that you wish to see him, sir ?

JOYCE.   Ong Chi Seng.

ONG CHI SENG (*turning*).   Yes, sir.

JOYCE.   Is there anything else you know ?

ONG CHI SENG.   No, sir.   I am of the opinion that a confidential clerk should have no secrets from his employer.   May I ask why you make this enquiry, sir ?

JOYCE.   Call Mr Crosbie.

ONG CHI SENG.   Very good, sir.

(*He turns and exits* R.   *After a few moments* CROSBIE *enters.*)

JOYCE (*rising*).   It's good of you to have waited, old man.

CROSBIE (*below the* R. *end of the table*).   Your clerk said that you particularly wanted me to.

JOYCE (*as casually as he can*).   A rather unpleasant thing has happened, Bob.   It appears that your wife sent a letter to Hammond asking him to come to the bungalow on the night he was killed.

CROSBIE.   But that's impossible.   She's always stated that she had had no communication with Hammond.   I know from my own knowledge that she hadn't set eyes upon him for a couple of months.

JOYCE (*moving* L. *of the table and below it*). The fact remains that the letter exits. It's in the possession of the Chinese woman Hammond was living with.

CROSBIE. What did she write to him for ?

JOYCE. Your wife meant to give you a present on your birthday, and she wanted Hammond to help her to get it. Your birthday was just about then, wasn't it ?

CROSBIE. Yes. In point of fact it was a fortnight ago today.

JOYCE. In the emotional excitement that she suffered from after the tragedy she forgot that she'd written a letter to him, and having once denied having any communication with Hammond she was afraid to say she'd made a mistake.

CROSBIE. Why ?

JOYCE. My dear fellow. It was, of course, very unfortunate, but I daresay it was not unnatural.

CROSBIE. That's unlike Leslie. I've never known her afraid of anything.

JOYCE. The circumstances were exceptional.

CROSBIE. Does it very much matter ? If she's asked about it she can explain.

JOYCE. It would be very awkward if this letter found its way into the hands of the prosecution. Your wife has lied, and she would be asked some difficult questions.

CROSBIE. Leslie would never tell a lie intentionally.

JOYCE (*with a shadow of impatience*). My dear Bob, you must try to understand. Don't you see that it alters things a good deal if Hammond did not intrude, an unwanted guest, but came to your house by invitation ? It would be easy to arouse in the jury a certain indecision of mind.

CROSBIE. I may be very stupid, but I don't understand. You lawyers, you seem to take a delight in making mountains out of mole-hills. After all, Howard, you're not only my lawyer, you're the oldest friend I have in the world.

JOYCE. I know. That is why I'm taking a step the gravity of which I can never expect you to realise. I think we must get hold of that letter. I want you to authorise me to buy it.

CROSBIE. I'll do whatever you think is right.

JOYCE (*turning and moving* L. *of the table to above it*). I don't think it's right, but I think it's expedient. Juries are very stupid. I think it's just as well not to worry them with more evidence than they can conveniently deal with.

CROSBIE. Well, I don't pretend to understand, but I'm perfectly prepared to leave myself in your hands. Go ahead and do as you think fit. I'll pay.

JOYCE (*collecting his papers*). All right. And now put the matter out of your mind.

CROSBIE. That's easy. I could never bring myself to believe

that Leslie had ever done anything that wasn't absolutely square and above board.

JOYCE (*moving to the door* L.). Let's go to the club. I badly want a whisky and soda.

They start to go as

the CURTAIN *falls*.

ACT III.

SCENE 1.

SCENE.—*A room in the Chinese quarter of Singapore. The same night.*

The room is small, with dirty and bedraggled whitewashed walls. Up C. *is a small window over which a dirty piece of lace curtain is roughly hung. There is a door* R. *The only furniture consists of a low Chinese pallet bed, with a lacquered neck-rest, with a stool* R. *of it and a low circular coffee table* L. *of it. On the floor,* L. *of the bed is a rattan sleeping mat, also with a neck-rest at the* R. *end. On the back wall are pinned a cheap Chinese oleograph, stained and discoloured, and a picture of a nude from one of the illustrated papers. The room is lit by one electric light, a globe without a shade.*

(See the Ground Plan at the end of the play.)

When the CURTAIN *rises,* CHUNG HI *is lying on the pallet bed with his opium pipe. On the table is a tray with a lighted spirit lamp, tin of opium and a couple of long needles. He is a fat Chinaman, in white trousers, singlet and Chinese slippers. He is reading a Chinese newspaper. A Chinese* BOY, *dressed in the same way, is sitting on the floor* C. *idly playing a Chinese flute. He plays a strange Chinese tune.* CHUNG HI *dips a needle in the tin of opium, extracts a small pellet and heating it over the spirit flame, puts it in his pipe. He inhales and presently blows out a thick cloud of smoke. There is a scratching at the door.* CHUNG HI *speaks a few words in Chinese and the* BOY *rises, moves to the door* R. *and opens it a little. He speaks to someone outside, then turns and says something in Chinese to* CHUNG HI, *who makes answer, rises and puts his opium pipe and paper down. The* BOY *opens the door wider and* ONG CHI SENG *enters.*

ONG CHI SENG. This way, sir, please. Come in.

*(*JOYCE *enters, wearing his topee. The* BOY *closes the door and sits on the stool* R.*)*

JOYCE *(crossing* L.*).* I nearly broke my neck on those stairs.
ONG CHI SENG. This is my friend, sir.
JOYCE. Does he speak English ?
CHUNG HI. Yes, my speakee velly good English. How do you do, sir. I hope you are quite well. Please to come in.
JOYCE. Good evening. I say, the air in here is awful. Couldn't we have the window open ?
CHUNG HI. Night air velly bad, sir. Him bring fever.
JOYCE. We'll risk it.

37

ONG CHI SENG (*crossing to the window*). Very good, sir. I will open the window. (*He does so.*)

JOYCE. I see you've been smoking.

CHUNG HI. Yes, my suffer velly bad from my belly. Smokee two, thlee pipes make it more better.

JOYCE. We'd better get to our business.

ONG CHI SENG. Yes, sir. Business is business, as we say.

JOYCE. What is your friend's name, Ong ?

CHUNG HI. My callee all same Chung Hi. You no see him written on shop ? Chung Hi. General Dealer ?

JOYCE. I suppose you know what I've come for ?

CHUNG HI. Yes, sir. My velly glad to see you in my house. Me give you my business card. Yes ?

JOYCE. I don't think I need it.

CHUNG HI. My sell you velly good China tea. All same Suchong. Number one quality. My can sell more cheap than you buy at stores.

JOYCE. I don't want any tea.

CHUNG HI. My sell you Swatow silk. Velly best quality. No can get more better in China. Make velly good suits. My sell you cheap.

JOYCE. I don't want any silk.

CHUNG HI. Velly well. You take my business card. Chung Hi, General Dealer, two-six-four, Victoria Street. Maybe you want some tomollow or next day.

JOYCE. Have you got this letter ?

CHUNG HI. Chinese woman have got.

JOYCE. Where is she ?

CHUNG HI. She come presently.

JOYCE. Why the devil isn't she here ?

CHUNG HI. She here all right. She come presently. She wait till you come. See ?

ONG CHI SENG. Much better you tell her to come, I think.

CHUNG HI. Yes, I tell her come this minute. (*He turns to the* BOY *and speaks to him in Chinese.*)

(*The* BOY *gives a guttural, monosyllabic reply, rises and exits* R.)

(*To* JOYCE.) You sit down. Yes ?

JOYCE. I prefer to stand.

CHUNG HI (*offering him a tin of cigarettes from the table*). You smokee cigarette. Velly good cigarette. All same Thlee Castles.

JOYCE. I don't want to smoke.

CHUNG HI. You wantchee buy China tea velly cheap. Number one quality.

JOYCE. Go to hell.

CHUNG HI. All light. My no savee. Maybe you likee Swatow silk. No ! You wantchee see jade ? Have got string number one quality. My sell you one thousand dollars. Velly nice plesent your missus.

JOYCE. Go to hell.

CHUNG HI. All light. I smokee cigarette. (*He takes a cigarette from the tin and lights it with the spirit lamp.*)

(*The* BOY *enters* R. *carrying a tray on which are three bowls of tea. He offers one to* JOYCE, *who shakes his head and turns away.* ONG CHI SENG *and* CHUNG HI *each take one. The* BOY *then sits on the stool* R.)

JOYCE. Why the devil doesn't this woman come ?

ONG CHI SENG. I think she come now, sir.

(*There is a scratching at the door.*)

JOYCE. I'm curious to see her.

(*The* BOY *rises and opens the door.*)

ONG CHI SENG. My fliend say that poor Mr Hammond, deceased, was completely under her thumb, sir.

CHUNG HI. She no speakee English. She speakee Malay and Chinese.

(*The* CHINESE WOMAN *enters. She wears a silk sarong and a long muslin coat over a blouse. On her arms are heavy gold bangles ; she wears a gold chain round her neck and gold pins in her shining, black hair. Her cheeks and mouth are painted, and she is heavily powdered ; arched eyebrows make a thin dark line over her eyes. She walks slowly to the pallet bed and sits on the edge of it with her legs dangling.* ONG CHI SENG *makes an observation to her in Chinese and she answers briefly. She takes no notice of* JOYCE.)

JOYCE. Has she got the letter ?

ONG CHI SENG. Yes, sir.

JOYCE. Where is it ?

ONG CHI SENG. She's a very ignorant woman, sir. I think she wants to see the money before she gives the letter.

JOYCE. Very well. (*He takes a bundle of notes from his pocket, counts them, and hands them to* ONG CHI SENG.)

(*The* CHINESE WOMAN *takes a cigarette from the tin and lights it. She appears to take no notice of what is proceeding.* ONG CHI SENG *counts the notes for himself, watched by* CHUNG HI. *All are grave and businesslike, the Chinese oddly unconcerned.*)

ONG CHI SENG. The sum is quite correct, sir.

(*The* CHINESE WOMAN *takes the letter from her tunic and hands it to* ONG CHI SENG.)

(*Glancing at the letter.*) This is the right document, sir. (*He hands it to* JOYCE.)

JOYCE (*taking the letter and reading it*). There's not very much for the money. (*He places it in his pocket.*)

ONG CHI SENG. I am sure you will not regret it, sir. Considering all the circumstances, it is what you call dirt cheap.

JOYCE (*ironically*). I know that you have too great a regard for me to allow me to pay more for an article than the market price.

ONG CHI SENG. Shall you want me for anything else tonight, please, sir ?

JOYCE. I don't think so.

ONG CHI SENG. In that case, sir, if it is convenient, I will stay here and talk to my friend.

JOYCE (*sardonically*). I suppose you want to divide the swag.

ONG CHI SENG. I am sorry, sir, that that is a word I have not come across in my studies.

JOYCE. You'd better look it out in the dictionary.

ONG CHI SENG. Yes, sir. I will do it without delay.

JOYCE. I have been wondering how much you were going to get out of this, Ong Chi Seng.

ONG CHI SENG. The labourer is worthy of his hire, as Our Lord said, sir.

JOYCE. I didn't know you were a Christian, Ong.

ONG CHI SENG. I am not, sir, to the best of my belief.

JOYCE. In that case he certainly isn't your Lord.

ONG CHI SENG. I was only making use of the common English idiom, sir. In point of fact, I am a disciple of the late Herbert Spencer. I have also been much influenced by Nietzche, Shaw and Herbert G. Wells.

JOYCE (*crossing to the door* R.). It is no wonder that I am no match for you.

He exits R. *as—*

the CURTAIN *falls.*

SCENE 2.

SCENE.—*The sitting-room at the Crosbies' bungalow. Next day. About five o'clock in the afternoon.*

The piano is closed and there are no flower bowls. The light is soft and mellow.

When the CURTAIN *rises the stage is empty, but immediately the sound is heard of a car arriving and stopping.* MRS JOYCE *and* WITHERS *enter by the verandah steps* L., *followed by the* HEAD-BOY *carrying a large basket, and another Chinese* SERVANT *carrying a suit-case.* MRS JOYCE *is a buxom, florid, handsome woman of about forty.*

MRS JOYCE (*coming below the stool* L., *looking around*). Good

gracious, how desolate the place looks. You can see in the twinkling
of an eye that there hasn't been a woman here to look after things.

WITHERS (*moving below the table*). I must say it does look a bit
dreary.

MRS JOYCE. I knew it. I felt it in my bones. That's why I
wanted to get here before Leslie. (*She turns and moves to the piano.*)
I thought we might have a chance to do a little something before she
came. (*She opens the piano and puts a piece of music from the top
on to the stand.*)

WITHERS. A few flowers would help.

MRS JOYCE. I wonder if these wretched boys will have had the
sense to pick some. (*She turns to the* HEAD-BOY.) Is the ice all
right, boy ?

HEAD-BOY. Yes, missy.

MRS JOYCE. Well, put it in some place where it won't melt.
Are there any flowers ?

HEAD-BOY. My lookee see.

MRS JOYCE (*to the Chinese* SERVANT). Oh, that's my bag. Put it
in the spare room.

(*The* HEAD-BOY *and the Chinese* SERVANT *exit with their loads* C.)

WITHERS (*seating himself* L. *of the table*). You know, I can't help
wondering how Mrs Crosbie can bring herself to come back here.
(*He takes out his pipe and lights it.*)

MRS JOYCE (*seating herself on the stool* L.). My poor friend, the
Crosbies' haven't got half a dozen houses to choose from. When
you've only one house I suppose you've got to live in it no matter
what's happened.

WITHERS. At all events I should have liked to wait a bit.

MRS JOYCE. I wanted her to. I'd made all my plans for them
both to come back to my house after the trial. I wanted them to
stay with me till they were able to get away for a holiday.

WITHERS. I should have thought that much the most sensible
thing to do.

MRS JOYCE. But they wouldn't. Bob said he couldn't leave the
estate, and Leslie said she couldn't leave Bob. So then I said
Howard and I would come down here. I thought it would be
easier for them if they had someone with them for a day or two.

WITHERS (*with a smile*). And I think you were determined not
to be robbed of your celebration.

MRS JOYCE (*gaily*). You don't know my million-dollar cocktails,
do you ? They're celebrated all through the F.M.S. When Leslie
was arrested I made a solemn vow that I wouldn't make another
until she was acquitted. I've been waiting for this day and no one
is going to deprive me of my treat.

WITHERS. Hence the ice, I suppose ?

MRS JOYCE. Hence the ice, wise young man. As soon as the
others come I'll start making them.

WITHERS. With your own hands ?

MRS JOYCE. With my own hands. I don't mind telling you I never knew anyone who could make a better cocktail than I can.

WITHERS (*with a grin*). We all think the cocktails we make ourselves better than anybody else's, you know.

MRS JOYCE (*merrily*). Yes, but you're all lamentably mistaken, and I happen to be right.

WITHERS. The ways of Providence are dark.

(*The* HEAD-BOY *and the Chinese* SERVANT *enter* C., *carrying bowls of flowers, which are placed, one on the table up* L., *one on the writing-desk* R., *and one on the piano.*)

MRS JOYCE. Oh, good. That makes the room look much more habitable.

WITHERS. They ought to be here in a minute.

MRS JOYCE. We went very fast, you know. And I daresay a good many people wanted to say a word or two to Leslie. I don't suppose they were able to get away as quickly as they expected.

(*The* HEAD-BOY *and the Chinese* SERVANT *exit* C.)

WITHERS. I'll wait till they come, shall I ?

MRS JOYCE. Of course you must wait.

WITHERS. I thought the Attorney-General was very decent.

MRS JOYCE. I knew he would be. I know his wife, you know. She said she thought Leslie should never be tried at all. But, of course, men are so funny.

WITHERS. I shall never forget the shout that when up when the jury came in and said, " Not guilty."

MRS JOYCE. It was thrilling, wasn't it ? And Leslie absolutely impassive, sitting there as though it had nothing to do with her.

WITHERS. I can't get over the way she gave her evidence. By George, she's a marvel.

MRS JOYCE. It was beautiful. I couldn't help crying. It was so modest and so restrained. Howard, who thinks me very hysterical and impulsive, told me the other day he'd never known a woman who had so much self-control as Leslie. And that's real praise, because I don't think he very much likes her.

WITHERS. Why not ?

MRS JOYCE. Oh, you know what men are. They never care very much for the women their particular friends marry.

(*The* HEAD-BOY *enters* C., *carrying the lace pillow, covered by a cloth.*)

WITHERS. Hulloa, what's this ?

HEAD-BOY. Missy pillow lace.

MRS JOYCE (*rising*). Oh, did you bring that ? (*She moves to him, and takes the cloth off.*)

HEAD-BOY. I thought maybe Missy wantchee. (*He puts the pillow down on the circular table as it was in* ACT I.)

MRS JOYCE.   I'm sure she will.   That was very thoughtful of you, boy.

(*The* HEAD-BOY *exits* C., *taking the cloth with him.*)

(*To* WITHERS.)   You know, sometimes you could kill these Chinese boys, and then all of a sudden they'll do things that are so kind and so considerate that you forgive them everything.

WITHERS (*rising and moving above the table to look at the lace*). By George, it is beautiful, isn't it ?   You know, it's just the sort of thing you'd expect her to do.

MRS JOYCE.   Mr Withers, I want to ask you something rather horrible.   When you came that night, where exactly was Geoff Hammond's body lying ?

WITHERS.   Out on the verandah, just under that lamp.   By God, it gave me a turn when I ran up the steps and nearly fell over him.

MRS JOYCE.   Has it occurred to you that every time Leslie comes into the house she'll have to step over the place where the body lay ? It's rather grim.

WITHERS.   Perhaps it won't strike her.

MRS JOYCE.   Fortunately she's not the sort of hysterical fool that I am.   But I . . .   Oh, dear, I could never sleep again.

(*There is the sound of a car approaching and stopping.*)

WITHERS (*turning to face the verandah*).   There they are.   They haven't been so long, after all.

MRS JOYCE (*turning and moving on to the verandah*).   No, they must have started within ten minutes of us.   (*She calls.*)   Leslie ! Leslie !   (*She turns, comes down into the room and moves down* L.C.)

(LESLIE *enters* C., *followed by* CROSBIE *and* JOYCE.   CROSBIE *is wearing a neat suit of ducks,* LESLIE *wears a silk wrap and a hat.*)

LESLIE (*moving down* L.C. *to* MRS JOYCE).   You haven't been here long, have you ?

(CROSBIE *crosses above the table and down* R.   JOYCE *seats himself in the chair* L. *of the table.*)

MRS JOYCE (*taking* LESLIE *in her arms*).   Welcome.   Welcome back to your home.

LESLIE (*releasing herself*).   Darling.   (*She looks around.*)   How nice and cosy it looks.   I can hardly realise that I've ever been away.

MRS JOYCE.   Are you tired ?   Would you like to go and lie down ?

LESLIE.   Tired ?   Why, I've been doing nothing but rest for the last six weeks.

MRS JOYCE.   Oh, Bob, aren't you happy to have her back again ?

JOYCE.   Now, Dorothy, don't gush, and if you must gush, gush over me.

MRS JOYCE.   I'm not going to gush over you, you old brute.

What have you done ?

LESLIE (*holding out her hand to* JOYCE, *with a charming smile*). He's done everything. I can never thank him enough. You don't know what he's been to me through all this dreary time of waiting. (*She shakes hands with* JOYCE.)

MRS JOYCE. I don't mind confessing that I thought you made rather a good speech, Howard.

JOYCE. Thank you for those kind words.

MRS JOYCE. I think perhaps you might have been a little more impassioned without hurting yourself.

WITHERS. I don't agree with you, Mrs Joyce. It's just because it was so cold and measured and business-like that it was so effective.

JOYCE. Let's have this drink you've been talking about, Dorothy.

MRS JOYCE (*moving up* C.). Come and help me, Mr Withers When I make a cocktail, I want a great many assistants.

LESLIE (*taking off her hat*). I know what an elaborate business your million dollar cocktail is, Dorothy.

MRS JOYCE. Don't be impatient. I can't hurry it. I must take my time.

(MRS JOYCE *and* WITHERS *exit* C.)

LESLIE. I'll go and tidy myself up.

CROSBIE. You don't need it. You look as if you'd just come out of a bandbox.

LESLIE. I shan't be a minute.

CROSBIE. There's something I particularly want to say to you.

JOYCE. I'll make myself scarce.

CROSBIE. No, I want you, old man. I want your legal opinion.

JOYCE. Oh, do you ? Fire away.

(LESLIE *puts her hat on the table and then sits on the stool* L.)

CROSBIE. Well, look here, I want to get Leslie away from here as quickly as possible.

JOYCE. I think a bit of a holiday would do you both good.

LESLIE. Could you get away, Robert ? Even if it's only for two or three weeks I'd be thankful.

CROSBIE. What's the use of two or three weeks ? We must get away for good.

LESLIE. But how can we ?

JOYCE. You can't very well throw up a job like this. You'd never get such a good one again, you know.

CROSBIE. That's where you're wrong. I've something in view that's much better. We can neither of us live here. It would be impossible. We've gone through too much in this bungalow. How can we ever forget . . . ?

LESLIE (*with a shudder*). No, don't, Bob, don't.

CROSBIE (*to* JOYCE). You see. Heaven knows, Leslie has nerves of iron, but there is a limit to human endurance. You know how lonely the life is.   I should never have a moment's peace when I was out and thought of her sitting in this room by herself.   It's out of the question.

LESLIE.   Oh, don't think of me, Bob.   You've made this estate, it was nothing when you came here.   Why, it's like your child. It's the apple of your eye.

CROSBIE.   I hate it now.   I hate every tree on it.   I must get away, and so must you.   You don't want to stay ?

LESLIE.   It's all been so miserable.   I don't want to make any more difficulties.

CROSBIE.   I know our only chance of peace is to get to some place where we can forget.

JOYCE.   But could you get another job ?

CROSBIE.   Yes, that's just it.   Something has suddenly cropped up.   That's why I wanted to talk to you about it at once.   It's in Sumatra.   We'd be right away from everybody, and the only people round us would be Dutch.   We'd start a new life, with new friends. The only thing is that you'd be awfully lonely, darling.

LESLIE.   Oh, I wouldn't mind that.   I'm used to loneliness. (*With sudden vehemence.*)   I'd be glad to go, Robert.   I don't want to stay here.

CROSBIE.   That settles it then.   I'll go straight ahead and we can fix things up at once.

JOYCE.   Is the money as good as here ?

CROSBIE.   I hope it'll be better.   At all events I shall be working for myself and not for a rotten company in London.

JOYCE (*startled*).   What do you mean by that ?   You're not buying an estate ?

CROSBIE.   Yes, I am.   Why should I go on sweating my life out for other people ?   It's a chance in a thousand.   It belongs to a Malacca Chinaman who's in financial difficulties, and he's willing to let it go for thirty thousand dollars if he can have the money the day after tomorrow.

JOYCE.   But how are you going to raise thirty thousand dollars ?

CROSBIE.   Well, I've saved about ten thousand since I've been in the East, and Charlie Meadows is willing to let me have the balance on mortgage.

(LESLIE *and* JOYCE *exchange a glance of consternation.*)

JOYCE.   It seems rather rash to put all your eggs in one basket.

LESLIE.   I shouldn't like you to take such a risk on my account, Robert.   You needn't worry about me, really.   I shall settle down here quite comfortably.

CROSBIE.   Don't talk nonsense, darling.   It's only a moment ago that you said you'd give anything to clear out.

LESLIE.   I spoke without thinking.   I believe it would be a mistake to run away.   The sensible thing to do is to sit tight. Everybody's been so kind, there's no reason to suppose they're not going to continue. I'm sure all our friends will do all they can to make things easy for us.

CROSBIE. You know, dear, you mustn't be frightened at a little risk. It's only if one takes risks that one can make big money.

JOYCE. These Chinese estates are never any good. You know how haphazard and careless the Chinese are.

CROSBIE. This is not that sort of thing at all. It belongs to a very progressive Chinaman, and he's had a European manager. It's not a leap in the dark. It's a thoroughly sound proposition, and I reckon that in ten years I can make enough money to allow us to retire. Then we'll settle down in England and live like lords.

LESLIE. Honestly, Robert, I'd prefer to stay here. I'm attached to the place, and when I've had time to forget all that has happened . . .

CROSBIE. How can you forget ?

JOYCE. Anyhow, it's not a thing that you must enter into without due consideration. You'd naturally want to go over to Sumatra and look for yourself.

CROSBIE. That's just it. I've got to make up my mind at once. The offer only holds for thirty-six hours.

JOYCE. But my dear fellow, you can't pay thirty thousand dollars for an estate without proper investigation. None of you planters are any too business-like, but really there are limits.

CROSBIE. Don't try to make me out a bigger fool than I am. I've had it examined and it's worth fifty thousand if it's worth a dollar. I've got all the papers in my office. I'll go and get them and you can see for yourself. And I have a couple of photographs of the bungalow to show Leslie.

LESLIE. I don't want to see them.

CROSBIE. Oh, come, darling. That's just nerves. That shows how necessary it is for you to get away. Darling, in this case you must let me have my own way. I want to go, too. I can't stay here any more.

LESLIE (*with anguish*). Oh, why are you so obstinate ?

CROSBIE (*moving to the door* R.). Come, come, dear, don't be unreasonable. Let me go and get the papers. I shan't be a minute.

(*He exits* R. *There is a moment's silence.* LESLIE *looks at* JOYCE *with terrified appeal ; he makes a despairing gesture.*)

JOYCE (*rising*). I had to pay ten thousand dollars for the letter.

LESLIE (*rising*). What are you going to do ?

JOYCE (*miserably*). What can I do ?

LESLIE. Oh, don't tell him now. Give me a little time. I'm at the end of my strength. I can't bear anything more.

JOYCE. You heard what he said. He wants the money at once to buy this estate. He can't. He hasn't got it.

LESLIE. Give me a little time.

JOYCE (*moving up* C.). I can't afford to give you a sum like that.

LESLIE. No, I don't expect you to. Perhaps I can get it somehow.

JOYCE (*turning*). How? You know it's impossible. It's money I put by for the education of my boys. I was glad to advance it, and I wouldn't have minded waiting a few weeks . . .

LESLIE (*interrupting*). If you'd only give me a month I'd have time to think of something. I could prepare Robert and explain to him by degrees. I'd watch for my opportunity.

JOYCE (*moving down* L. *of* LESLIE). If he buys this estate the money will be gone. No, no, no. I can't let him do that. I don't want to be unkind to you, but I can't lose my money.

LESLIE. Where is the letter?

JOYCE. I have it in my pocket.

LESLIE (*sitting* L. *of the table*). Oh, what shall I do?

JOYCE. I'm dreadfully sorry for you.

LESLIE. Oh, don't be sorry for me. I don't matter. It's Robert. It'll break his heart.

JOYCE. If there were only some other way. I don't know what to do. (*He sits despondently on the stool* L.)

LESLIE. I suppose you're right. There's only one thing to do. Tell him. Tell him and have done with it. I'm broken.

(CROSBIE *enters* R., *carrying a bundle of papers*.)

CROSBIE (*crossing above the table to* C.). Of course if it hadn't been for Leslie I should have run over to Sumatra last week. I'd just like you to have a look first at the report I've had.

JOYCE. Look here, Bob, has it struck you that your costs over this affair will be pretty heavy?

CROSBIE. I know all you lawyers are robbers. I daresay this will leave me a little short of money, but I don't suppose you'll mind if I keep you waiting till I've had time to settle down. You know I can be trusted, and if you like I'll pay you interest.

JOYCE. I don't think you have any idea how large the sum is. Of course, we don't want to press you, but we can't be out of our money indefinitely. I think I should warn you that when you've settled with us, you won't have much money left over to embark in rather hazardous speculations.

CROSBIE. You're putting the fear of God into me. How much will the costs come to?

JOYCE. I'm not going to charge you anything for my personal services. Whatever I've done has been done out of pure friendship, but there are certain out-of-pocket expenses that I'm afraid you must pay.

CROSBIE. Of course. It's awfully good of you not to wish to charge me for anything else. I hardly like to accept. What do the out-of-pocket expenses amount to?

JOYCE. You remember that I told you yesterday that there was a letter of Leslie's that I thought we ought to get hold of.

CROSBIE. Yes, I really didn't think it mattered very much, but, of course, I put myself in your hands. I thought you were making a great deal out of something that wasn't very important.

JOYCE. You told me to do what I thought fit, and I bought the letter from the person in whose possession it was. I had to pay a great deal of money for it.

CROSBIE. What a bore. Still, if you thought it necessary, I'm not going to grouse. How much was it ?

JOYCE. I'm afraid I had to pay ten thousand dollars for it.

CROSBIE (aghast). Ten thousand dollars ! Why, that's a fortune. I thought you were going to say a couple of hundred. You must have been mad.

JOYCE. You may be sure that I wouldn't have given it if I could have got it for less.

CROSBIE. But that's everything I have in the world. It reduces me to beggary.

JOYCE. Not that exactly, but you must understand that you haven't got money to buy an estate with.

CROSBIE. But why didn't you let them bring the letter in and tell them to do what they damned well liked ?

JOYCE. I didn't dare.

CROSBIE. Do you mean to say it was absolutely necessary to suppress the letter ?

JOYCE. If you wanted your wife acquitted.

CROSBIE. But—but . . . I don't understand. You're not going to tell me that they could have brought in a verdict of guilty. They couldn't have hanged her for putting a noxious vermin out of the way.

JOYCE. Of course, they wouldn't have hanged her. But they might have found her guilty of manslaughter. I daresay she'd have got off with two or three years.

CROSBIE. Three years. My Leslie. My little Leslie. It would have killed her. But what was there in the letter ?

JOYCE. I told you yesterday.

LESLIE. It was very stupid of me. I . . .

CROSBIE (interrupting). I remember now. You wrote to Hammond to ask him to come to the bungalow.

LESLIE. Yes.

CROSBIE. You wanted him to get something for you, didn't you ?

LESLIE. Yes, I wanted to get a present for your birthday.

CROSBIE. Why should you have asked him ?

LESLIE. I wanted to get you a gun. He knew all about that sort of thing, and you know how ignorant I am.

CROSBIE. Bertie Cameron had a brand new gun he wanted to sell. I went into Singapore on the night of Hammond's death to buy it. Why should you want to make me a present of another ?

LESLIE. How should I know that you were going to buy a gun ?

CROSBIE (abruptly). Because I told you.

LESLIE. I'd forgotten. I can't remember everything.

CROSBIE. You hadn't forgotten that.

LESLIE. What do you mean, Robert ? Why are you talking to me like this ?

CROSBIE (*to* JOYCE). Wasn't it a criminal offence that you committed in buying that letter ?

JOYCE (*trying not to take it seriously*). It's not the sort of thing that a respectable lawyer does in the ordinary way of business.

CROSBIE (*pressing him*). It was a criminal offence ?

JOYCE. I've been trying to keep the fact out of my mind. But if you must insist on a straight answer I'm afraid I must admit it was.

CROSBIE. Then why did you do it ? You, you of all people. What were you trying to save me from ?

JOYCE. Well, I've told you. I felt that . . .

CROSBIE (*hard and stern*). No, you haven't.

JOYCE. Come, come, Bob, don't be a fool. I don't know what you mean. Juries are very stupid, and you don't want them to get any silly ideas in their heads.

CROSBIE. Who has the letter now ? Have you got it ?

JOYCE. Yes.

CROSBIE. Where is it ?

JOYCE. Why do you want to know ?

CROSBIE (*violently*). God damn it, I want to see it.

JOYCE (*rising*). I've no right to show it you.

CROSBIE (*violently*). Is it your money you bought it with, or mine ? I've got to pay ten thousand dollars for that letter, and by God I'm going to see it. At least I'd like to know that I've had my money's worth.

LESLIE. Let him see it.

(*Without a word* JOYCE *takes his pocket-book from his pocket and extracts the letter which he hands to* CROSBIE, *who reads it.*)

CROSBIE (*hoarsely*). What does it mean ? (*He breaks down* L.)

LESLIE. It means that Geoff Hammond was my lover.

CROSBIE (*covering his face with his hands*). No, no.

JOYCE. Why did you kill him ?

LESLIE (*rising*). He'd been my lover for years. (*She moves down* R.C.)

CROSBIE (*in agony*). It's not true.

LESLIE (*turning*). For years. And then he changed. I didn't know what was the matter. I couldn't believe that he didn't care for me any more. I loved him ; I didn't want to love him. I couldn't help myself. I hated myself for loving him, and yet he was everything in the world to me. He was all my life. And then I heard that he was living with a Chinese woman. I couldn't believe it. At last I saw her, I saw her with my own eyes, walking in the village, with her gold bracelets and her necklaces—a Chinese woman. Horrible ! They all knew in the kampong that she was his mistress.

And when I passed her, she looked at me, and I saw that she knew I was his mistress, too. I sent for him.

(*The* LIGHTS *fade to blackout. When the* LIGHTS *come up again,* LESLIE *is seated* R. *of the table working at her lace. She is dressed as in* ACT I. *It is night, and the lamps are lit.* GEOFFREY HAMMOND *enters up the verandah steps.· He is a good-looking fellow in the late thirties, with a breezy manner and abundant self-confidence.*)

LESLIE (*rising and placing the lace pillow on the table*). Geoff ! I thought you were never coming.

HAMMOND (*moving down* C.). What's that bold bad husband of yours gone to Singapore for ?

· LESLIE. He's gone to buy a gun that Bertie Cameron wants to sell.

HAMMOND. I suppose he wants to bag that tiger the natives are talking about. I bet I get him first. What about a little drink ?

LESLIE. Help yourself.

(HAMMOND *turns and moves to the table up* L.)

HAMMOND (*pouring out a whisky and soda*). I say, is anything the matter ? That note of yours was rather hectic.

LESLIE. What have you done with it ?

HAMMOND (*turning and moving* C. *with his drink*). I tore it up at once. What do you take me for ?

LESLIE (*suddenly*). Geoff, I can't go on like this any more. I'm at the end of my tether.

HAMMOND. Why, what's up ?

LESLIE. Oh, don't pretend. What's the good of that ? Why have you left me all this time without a sign ?

HAMMOND. I've had an awful lot to do. (*He drinks and then returns his glass to the table up* L.)

LESLIE. You haven't had so much to do that you couldn't spare a few minutes to write to me.

HAMMOND (*moving down* C.). There didn't seem to be any object in taking useless risks. If we don't want a bust-up, we must take elementary precautions. We've been very lucky so far. It would be silly to make a mess of things now.

LESLIE. Don't treat me like a perfect fool.

HAMMOND. I say, Leslie, darling, if you sent for me just to make a scene, I'm going to take myself off. I'm sick of these eternal rows.

LESLIE. A scene ? Don't you know how I love you ?

HAMMOND. Well, darling, you've got a damned funny way of showing it.

LESLIE. You drive me to desperation.

(HAMMOND *looks at her for a moment reflectively, then, with his hands in his pockets, goes up to her with deliberation.*)

· HAMMOND. Leslie, I wonder if you've noticed that we hardly ever meet now without having a row.

LESLIE.   Is that my fault ?

HAMMOND.   I don't say that.   I daresay it's mine.   But when that happened with two people who are on the sort of terms that we are, it looks very much as though things were wearing a bit thin.

LESLIE.   What do you mean by that ?

HAMMOND.   Well, when that happens, I'm not sure if the common-sense thing is not to say : " We've had a ripping time, but all good things must come to an end, and the best thing we can do is to make a break while we've still got the chance of keeping friends."

LESLIE (*frightened*).   Geoff !

HAMMOND.   I'm all for facing facts.

LESLIE (*suddenly flaming up*).   Facts !   What is that Chinawoman doing in your house ?

HAMMOND.   My dear, what are you talking about ?

LESLIE.   Do you think I don't know that you've been living with a Chinawoman for months ?

HAMMOND.   Nonsense.

LESLIE.   What sort of a fool do you take me for ?   Why, it's the gossip of the kampong.

HAMMOND (*with a shrug of the shoulders*).   My dear, if you're going to listen to the gossip of the natives . . .

LESLIE (*interrupting him*).   Then what is she doing in your bungalow ?

HAMMOND (*turning and moving up* C.).   I didn't know there was a Chinawoman about.   I don't bother much about what goes on in my servants' quarters as long as they do their work properly.

LESLIE (*seating herself* L. *of the table*).   What does that mean ?

HAMMOND (*turning*).   Well, I shouldn't be surprised if one of the boys had got a girl there.   What do I care as long as she keeps out of my way.

LESLIE.   I've seen her.

HAMMOND (*moving down to* R. *of her*).   What is she like ?

LESLIE.   Old and fat.

HAMMOND.   You're not paying me a very pretty compliment. My head-boy's old and fat, too.

LESLIE.   Your head-boy isn't going to dress a woman in silk at five dollars a yard.   She had a couple of hundred pounds' worth of jewellery on her.

HAMMOND.   It sounds as though she were of a thrifty disposition. Perhaps she thinks that the best way to invest her savings.

LESLIE.   Will you swear she's not your mistress ?

HAMMOND.   Certainly.

LESLIE.   On your honour ?

HAMMOND.   On my honour.

LESLIE (*violently*).   It's a lie.

HAMMOND.   All right, then, it's a lie.   But in that case, why won't you let me go ?

LESLIE.   Because, in spite of everything, I love you with all my heart.   I can't let you go now.   You're all I have in the world.   If you have no love for me, have pity on me.   Without you I'm lost. Oh, Geoff, I love you.   No one will ever love you as I've loved you. I know that often I've been beastly to you and horrible, but I've been so unhappy.

HAMMOND.   My dear, I don't want to make you unhappy, but it's no good beating about the bush.   The thing's over and done with.   You must let me go now.   You really must.

LESLIE (*rising*).   Oh no, 'Geoff, you don't mean that, you can't mean that.

HAMMOND.   Leslie, dear, I'm terribly sorry, but the facts are there and you've got to face them.   This is the end and you've got to make the best of it.   I've made up my mind, and there it is. (*He crosses down* L.)

LESLIE.   How cruel.   How monstrously cruel.   You wouldn't treat a dog as you're treating me.

HAMMOND (*turning*).   Is it my fault if I don't love you ?   Damn it all, one either loves or one doesn't.

LESLIE.   Oh, you're of stone.   I'd do anything in the world for you, and you won't give me a chance.

HAMMOND (*moving to her*).   Oh, my God, why can't you be reasonable ?   I tell you I'm sick and tired of the whole thing.   Do you want me to tell you in so many words that you mean nothing to me ?   Don't you know that ?   Haven't you felt it ?   You must be blind.

LESLIE (*desperately*).   Yes, I've known it only too well.   And I've felt it.   I didn't care.   It's not love any more that seethes in my heart ; it's madness ; it's torture to see you, but it's torture ten times worse not to see you.   If you leave me now, I'll kill myself. (*She picks up the revolver that is lying on the table*.)   I swear to God I'll kill myself.

HAMMOND (*impatiently*).   Oh, don't talk such damned rot !

LESLIE.   Don't you think I mean it ?   Don't you think I have the courage ?

HAMMOND (*beside himself with irritation*).   I have no patience with you.   You're enough to drive anyone out of his senses.   If you'd got sick of me, would you have hesitated to send me about my business ?   Not for a minute.   D'you think I don't know women ?

LESLIE (*replacing the revolver on the table*).   You've ruined my life, and now you're tired of me you want to cast me aside like a worn-out coat.   No, no, no !

HAMMOND.   You can do what you like, and say what you like, but I tell you it's finished.

LESLIE (*flinging her arms round his neck*).   I'll never let you go. Never !   Never !

(HAMMOND *releases himself roughly. The touch of her exasperates him.*)

HAMMOND (*thrusting her away*). I'm fed up. Fed up. I'm sick of the sight of you.

LESLIE (*collapsing into the chair* R. *of the table*). No, no, no.

HAMMOND (*violently*). If you want the truth you must have it. (*He stands over her.*) Yes, the Chinawoman is my mistress, and I don't care who knows it. If you ask me to choose between you and her, I choose her. Every time. (*He breaks* C. *and turns.*) And now for God's sake leave me alone.

LESLIE (*rising*). You cur ! (*She seizes the revolver and fires at him.*)

(HAMMOND *staggers towards the verandah and falls.*)

(*The* LIGHTS *quickly fade to Blackout.*)

I ran after him and fired again. He fell, and then I stood over him and I fired till there were no more cartridges.

(*The* LIGHTS *come up again.* CROSBIE *is now down* L. *and* JOYCE *up* C. *They are listening to* LESLIE'S *story. She is dressed as at the beginning of the scene.*)

CROSBIE. Have I deserved this of you, Leslie ? (*He moves to the stool* L. *and sits.*)

LESLIE. No, I have no excuses to offer for myself. I betrayed you.

CROSBIE. What do you want to do now ?

LESLIE (*rising*). It is for you to say.

CROSBIE. How could you, Leslie ? The awful part is that, not-withstanding everything—I love you still. Oh, God, how you must despise me. I despise myself.

(LESLIE *shakes her head slowly.*)

LESLIE (*crossing to* CROSBIE *and putting her hand across his shoulders*). I don't know what I've done to deserve your love. Oh, if only I could blame anybody but myself. I can't. I deserve everything I have to suffer. Oh, Robert, my dear.

(CROSBIE *buries his head in his hands.*)

CROSBIE. Oh, what shall I do ? It's all gone. All gone. (*He begins to sob with the great, painful, difficult sobs of a man unused to tears.*)

LESLIE (*sinking on her knees beside him*). Oh, don't cry. My dear —my dear.

(CROSBIE *pushes her on one side and springs up.*)

CROSBIE (*crossing to the door* R.). I'm a fool. There's no need for me to make an exhibition of myself. I'm sorry.

(*He exits* R.   LESLIE *rises*.)

JOYCE (*moving down* C.). No. Don't go to him. Give him a moment to get hold of himself.

LESLIE.   I'm so dreadfully sorry for him.

JOYCE.   He's going to forgive you. He can't do without you.

LESLIE.   If only he'd give me another chance.

JOYCE.   Don't you love him at all ?

LESLIE.   No. I wish to God I did.

JOYCE.   Then what's to be done ?

LESLIE.   I swear to you that I'll do everything in the world to make him happy. I'll make amends. I'll oblige him to forget. He shall never know that I don't love him as he wants to be loved.

JOYCE.   It's not easy to live with a man you don't love. But you've had the courage and the strength to do evil ; perhaps you will have the courage and the strength to do good. That will be your retribution.

LESLIE.   No, that won't be my retribution. I can do that and do it gladly. He's so kind and good. My retribution is greater. With all my heart I still love the man I killed.

CURTAIN.

FURNITURE AND PROPERTY PLOT.

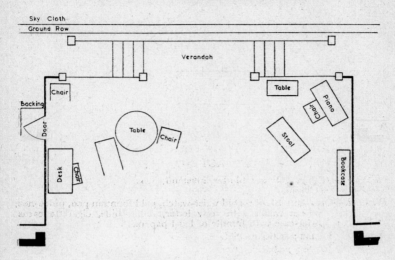

ACT I.

On Stage.—Rattan armchair with extending leg-rest.   *On it:* cushion.
　　　　2 Rattan armchairs.   *On them :* cushions.
　　　　2 small rattan chairs.
　　　　Circular table.   *On it :* lamp, lace pillow, revolver, pair of
　　　　　　　　　　　spectacles, box of cigarettes, matches,
　　　　　　　　　　　ashtray.
　　　　Writing desk.   *On it :* blotter, inkstand, pens and pencils,
　　　　　　　　　　　writing paper, bowl of flowers.
　　　　Bookcase.
　　　　Occasional table.   *On it :* bowl of flowers, tray with bottle of
　　　　　　　　　　　whisky, soda, glasses.
　　　　Piano.   *On it :* lamp, ornaments, bowl of flowers, music—one
　　　　　　　　　　　piece on stand.
　　　　Long stool.
　　　　Rattan mats.
　　　　On the walls : water-colours, native weapons, hunting trophies.
　　　　Hanging lamp (over verandah.)

Off Stage R.—Hat and coat (LESLIE).

Personal.—CROSBIE : handkerchief in L. pocket of jacket.

Motor-car effects.

Lamps lit.

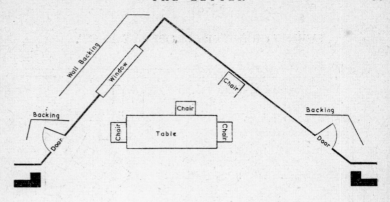

ACT II.

On Stage.—Table. *On it :* blotter, inkstand, pens.
4 Chairs.

Personal.—ONG CHI SENG : gold wrist-watch, gold fountain pen, pince-nez,
pocket wallet with copy letter, dollar bills, cigarette cards,
brief-case with bundle of legal papers.

LESLIE : handkerchief.

JOYCE : watch.

ACT III.

SCENE 1.

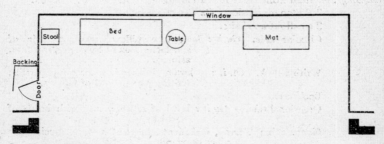

On Stage.—Pallet Bed.

Stool.

Coffee table. *On it :* opium pipe, tin of cigarettes, tray with
lighted spirit lamp, tin of opium, two
needles.

Rattan sleeping mat.

2 Chinese neck-rests.

Off Stage.—Tray. *On it :* 3 bowls of tea (CHINESE BOY).

Personal.—CHUNG HI : Chinese newspaper.

JOYCE : wallet with bundle of Chinese dollar notes.

CHINESE WOMAN : letter.

SCENE 2.

On Stage.—Furniture, etc., as ACT I.   But no flower bowls and pillow lace.
Piano closed, music on top.

Off Stage.—Suit Case (CHINESE SERVANT).
Basket of ice (HEAD-BOY).
3 Bowls of flowers (HEAD-BOY and CHINESE SERVANT).
Lace pillow covered with cloth (HEAD-BOY).

Off Stage R.—Bundle of papers (CROSBIE).

Personal.—JOYCE : wallet with letter.
WITHERS : pipe, tobacco, matches.
During Black-Out *Strike*—LESLIE'S hat.
Set   —Revolver on table.
During 2nd Black-Out *Strike*—Revolver.
Set   —LESLIE'S hat.

Motor-car effects.

LIGHTING PLOT.

ACT I.—Night.

Floods on backcloth. 32 Blue.

Spots to cover the areas presumed to be lit by the lamps.—3 Straw.

Floats and Battens $\begin{cases} \text{4 Amber.} \\ \text{36 Lavender.} \\ \text{White.} \end{cases}$

All full up to open.

Cue 1. HEAD-BOY turns out lamp on piano—spots covering area presumed to be lit by piano lamps OUT. Check Battens and Floats to ½.

Cue 2. HEAD-BOY turns out lamp on table—remaining Spots OUT. Battens and Floats OUT.

ACT II.—Morning.

Flood on wall outside window.—White.

Float and Battens.—White.

All full up.

No cues.

ACT III. SCENE 1.—Night.

Flood outside window. 32 Blue.

Floats and Battens.—White checked to ½.

No cues.

SCENE 2.—Late afternoon.

Floods on backcloth. 4 Amber.

Floats and Battens $\begin{cases} \text{4 Amber.} \\ \text{36 Lavender.} \end{cases}$

All full up to open.

Cue 1. LESLIE : " I sent for him."—Quick fade out to Black-out.

Cue 2. Fade in opening lighting of ACT I.

Cue 3. HAMMOND staggers and falls.—Quick fade to Black-out.

Cue 4. LESLIE : " I fired till there were no more cartridges."—Fade in opening lighting of ACT III, SCENE 2.